D0906117

The Mysterious  & Unknown

Stonehenge

by Toney Allman

ReferencePoint Press™

San Diego, CA

For more information, contact:
ReferencePoint Press, Inc.
PO Box 27779
San Diego, CA 92198
www.ReferencePointPress.com

Picture credits:
Cover: Dreamstime
Maury Aaseng, 7, 10, 26, 27, 29, 39, 61 63
AP/Wide World Photos, 31
IStock Photo, 13
Landov, 48
North Wind, 16, 18, 51, 54, 70
Photos.com, 12
Science Photo Library, 6, 27 79

Series design:
Amy Stirnkorb

LIBRARY OF CONGRESS CATALOGING-IN-PUBLICATION DATA

Allman, Toney.
Stonehenge / by Toney Allman.
p. cm.—(Mysterious & unknown series)
Includes bibliographical references and index.
ISBN-13: 978-1-60152-034-0 (hardback)
ISBN-10: 1-60152-034-4 (hardback)
1. Stonehenge (England)—Juvenile literature. 2. Wiltshire (England)—Antiquities—Juvenile literature. 3. Megalithic monuments—England—Wiltshire—Juvenile literature. I. Title.
 DA142.A45 2008
 936.2'319—dc22

2007028658

CONTENTS

FOREWORD

"Strange is our situation here upon earth."
—*Albert Einstein*

Since the beginning of recorded history, people have been perplexed, fascinated, and even terrified by events that defy explanation. While science has demystified many of these events, such as volcanic eruptions and lunar eclipses, some remain outside the scope of the provable. Do UFOs exist? Are people abducted by aliens? Can some people see into the future? These questions and many more continue to puzzle, intrigue, and confound despite the enormous advances of modern science and technology.

It is these questions, phenomena, and oddities that Reference-Point Press's *The Mysterious & Unknown* series is committed to exploring. Each volume examines historical and anecdotal evidence as well as the most recent theories surrounding the topic in debate. Fascinating primary source quotes from scientists, experts, and eyewitnesses as well as in-depth sidebars further inform the text. Full-color illustrations and photos add to each book's visual appeal. Finally, source notes, a bibliography, and a thorough index provide further reference and research support. Whether for research or the curious reader, *The Mysterious & Unknown* series is certain to satisfy those fascinated by the unexplained.

INTRODUCTION

Silent Stones

When author Bernard Cornwell was a little boy growing up in England, his parents took him to see Stonehenge. He still remembers wandering around the ancient stones and feeling a sense of awe and wonder. He knew it was an important part of British history, but he also knew that it was an unexplained mystery. It is a marvel of complex engineering—the only stone monument built in the ancient world with a lintel (a horizontal crosspiece, like a beam) across the tops of the upraised stones. Erected thousands of years ago, it offers few clues about its builders or its purpose.

When he grew up, Cornwell remained fascinated by the towering ruins, and in 2004 he wrote a historical novel titled simply *Stonehenge*, which tries to make the monument come to life. He had to imagine what the people were like and why they built Stonehenge, because no one knows the true story. Cornwell explains, "When you visit Stonehenge there's nothing there that really tells you what it is, . . . There's a good deal of information about how it was done and virtually nothing about why."[1]

"What is it?" The question has been asked by generations of people and answered in dozens of different ways. Stonehenge

Did You Know?

Stonehenge is the only stone monument built in the ancient world with a lintel across the tops of the upraised stones.

Stonehenge is located on Salisbury Plain in Wiltshire, England. It is thought to have been erected around 2100 B.C.

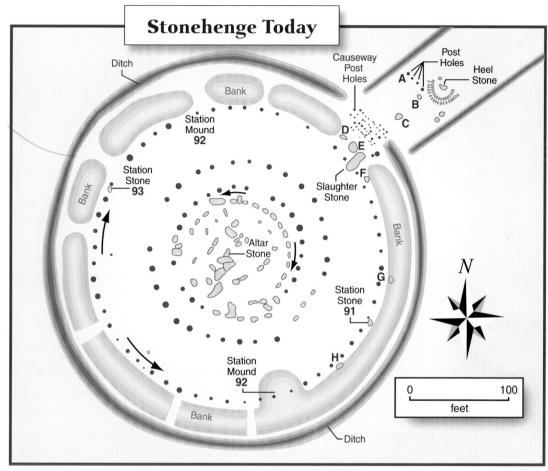

Stonehenge Today

Ditch

Causeway
Post
Holes

Post
Holes

Heel
Stone

A

B

C

Bank

Station
Mound
92

D

E

Station
Stone
93

F

Slaughter
Stone

Bank

Bank

Altar
Stone

N

Station
Stone
91

G

Station
Mound
92

H

Bank

0   100

feet

Ditch

expert R.J.C. Atkinson responds, "There is one short, simple and perfectly correct answer: We do not know and shall probably never know."[2] But ignorance has not prevented speculation. Stonehenge has come to mean many things to many different generations of people. Some theories are mystical, and some are scientific, but none are any more than guesses. Through it all, the stones stand silently and keep their secrets to themselves.

This diagram shows the key parts of Stonehenge, including the Heel Stone and the Altar Stone.

CHAPTER 1

Mysterious Stonehenge

Some of the huge stones have fallen over; some have been cracked apart and carted away; but many gigantic stone pillars still reach for the sky. They are the remnants of the amazing ring of stones known as Stonehenge. On the almost-desert of the Salisbury Plain in southern England, the broken circle of stones looms startlingly and enigmatically, the highest structure the eye can see for miles in every direction. For thousands of years generations of visitors have gazed and wondered, What is this place, and who erected it on this lonesome plain?

The Ring of Stones

The standing stones of Stonehenge are called megaliths. They are large blocks of stone that have been partially shaped and chipped into tall pillars, with one end buried deep in the ground. An outer ring of 30 of these stones was erected to form a partial circle 108 feet (33m) in diameter. Laid across the tops of the megaliths were 30 stones that formed a lintel, or crosspiece. The lintel rests on standing stones that are 13.5 feet (4.1m) tall, 7.5 feet (2.1m) wide, and weigh an average of 25 tons (23t) each. The stones that form the lintel are about 10.5 feet (3.2m) long, 2.75 feet (0.8m) thick, and 3.5 feet (1m) wide. The stones are not just balanced in their positions. Each one has been carved with joints, like mortise and tenon joints in wood, so that they fit together. At the top of each megalith a knob has been carved out; this is the tenon part. The underside of the lintel has a chipped-out hole (the mortise) that fits over the knob. The lintel stones also have tongues and grooves to link them together. All these outer stones are called sarsen stones. Sarsen is a kind of sandstone, and such huge sandstone boulders are found naturally on England's Salisbury Plain.

Patterns in Sarsen and Bluestone

The stones do not form a complete circle; rather the circle is left open, perhaps on purpose or perhaps because the remaining stones were removed at some point in history. But more is inside the unfinished sarsen circle: two horseshoes of other remarkable stones. The outer horseshoe was at one time an arrangement of 5 trilithons—2 standing stones with a crosspiece on top. The largest of these trilithons is the only one still standing today. Its bases are buried 8 feet (2.4m) in the ground, yet it still rises 20 feet (6m) into the air. This Great Trilithon is formed by stones weighing about 50 tons (45t) each. The other Stonehenge horseshoe, inside the trilithons, is called the Bluestone Horseshoe because of the bluish tint of the stones. The bluestones are not capped with lintels but stand alone. At one time a circle of bluestones stood between the sarsen stones, but today only 6 are still standing

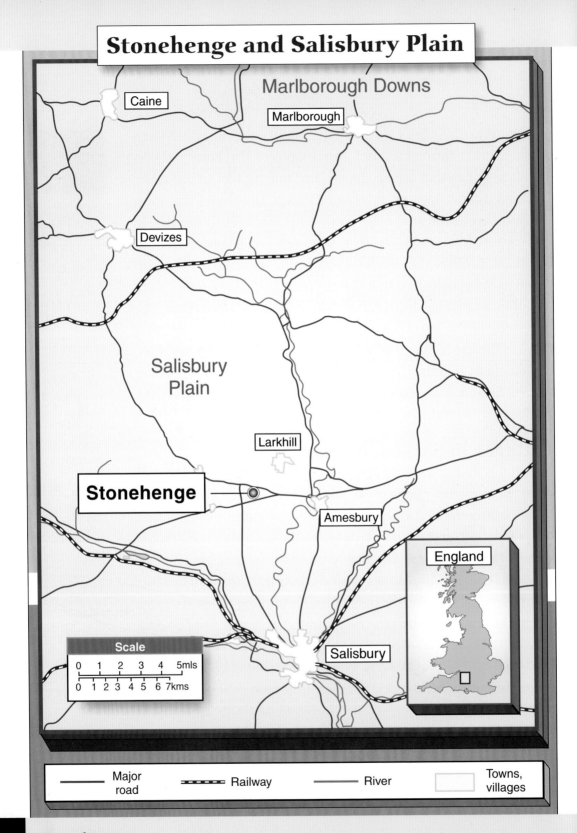

Stonehenge and Salisbury Plain

Marlborough Downs

Caine

Marlborough

Devizes

Salisbury
Plain

Larkhill

Stonehenge —

Amesbury

England

Salisbury

Scale

| 0 | 1 | 2 | 3 | 4 | 5mls |
| 0 | 1 | 2 | 3 | 4 | 5 | 6 | 7kms |

| —— | Major road | ┅┅ | Railway | —— | River | ▢ | Towns, villages |

erect. The others have tilted or fallen or disappeared.

As complex as this stone arrangement is, yet more can be seen. The horseshoes are open toward the northeast. At the center of the inner curve of the inner horseshoe is a stone slab called the Altar Stone which is partially buried in the earth and is a greenish sandstone that glitters with mica. It is 16 feet (4.9m) long. Standing 100 feet (30.5m) outside the circle, where the horseshoes are open and the 35-foot-wide entrance (10.7m) to the monument seems to have been, is a 35-ton sarsen stone (32t) named the Heel Stone. Originally it probably stood erect but leans inward at a 30-degree angle today. And even more can be found, but the monument must be studied carefully to find it. Outside the whole stone monument, weathered and eroded by wind and time, are 2 circling embankments with a ditch in between. Just inside the inner mound are 56 evenly spaced holes. A broad avenue with banks on either side runs from the Avon River, about 2 miles (3.2km) away, to the entrance to Stonehenge. A few other giant stones lie or stand around Stonehenge, including one now called the Slaughter stone.

Incredible Age

No one can walk up the Avenue to Stonehenge without being impressed. It represents an amazing amount of work and building skill. Yet for centuries no one could imagine who could have erected such a structure, or how ancient it was, or what its purpose was. Stonehenge's builders apparently abandoned the monument by about 1100 B.C. They left no written records of themselves, not even pictures drawn on the stones. They were lost and forgotten in time, unknown to the people who came after them. Their language had disappeared, and not even the true name they gave to Stonehenge survived. No one had any idea how the strange and

The standing stones of Stonehenge are called megaliths. They are large blocks of stone that have been partially shaped and chipped into tall pillars, with one end buried deep in the ground. Laid across the tops of the megaliths were 30 stones that formed a lintel, or crosspiece.

wonderful Stonehenge ruin came to be. It just seemed to have always been there, brooding alone on the Salisbury Plain.

Salisbury Plain is a plateau of chalk beds. Even today it is a relatively barren place with a small population. Although sarsen stones lie naturally on the surface within about 20 miles (32.2km) of Stonehenge, bluestones are nowhere to be found. The closest place where bluestones can be quarried is in the Prescelly Mountains of Wales, 130 miles (209km) distant. Could people of prehistory—before the wheel or written language had been invented—have hauled, shaped, and erected the stones of this monument? Could they have planned and built the towering monument in all its detail? For many centuries the answer was a definite "no." In awe but with a determination to explain, people told the stories of how they thought Stonehenge came to be.

Myth of the Heel Stone

Through one such myth, the Heel Stone got its name. According to the legend, the stones are magical, and no one can count all the stones. The devil had bought the magical stones from an old Irish woman. He carried them through the air and placed them on the Salisbury Plain. Then he approached the people of a nearby village and bet them that they could not count the stones. A monk or friar in the village had an answer for the devil. He said there were "more than could be told."[3] Since this was correct, the devil was furious to have his riddle solved. He picked up the giant stone and threw it at the fleeing friar. The friar was unhurt, but the stone nicked his heel as he ran away. The mark of his heel can be seen to this day as a dent in the upright Heel Stone.

Some archeologists and historians have another explanation for the Heel Stone. It is a stone with an impressive position. At the point in midsummer when the day is the longest, the sun rises directly over the top of the Heel Stone when viewed from inside

Did You Know?

Salisbury Plain is a plateau of chalk beds.

The Heel Stone, pictured, got its name from a myth about the devil striking a friar's heel with the stone.

Stonehenge. This time is called the summer solstice, and it may have been a date of great importance to the builders. The stone was placed so that the first rays of the sun on that day appeared behind it and the full sun at dawn seemed to hover atop the stone. An ancient Anglo-Saxon word for "hidden" is *helan*. (The Angles and the Saxons were two groups of European peoples who migrated to Britain in the 5th and 6th centuries A.D. Anglo-Saxons are some of the ancestors of the British people.) Perhaps, say the scientists, "heel" is a corruption of the word *helan* and refers to the sun being hidden behind the stone till it has fully risen.

Magic Stones

Stonehenge may have been a place of sun worship and magic. Another legend of Stonehenge says that the megaliths were once giants. As they danced together, holding hands, they were caught by a sunbeam and turned to stone. So the correct name of Stonehenge is "Giants' Ring" or "Giants' Dance."

Throughout early history, magic was connected with the myths of Stonehenge. In some legends the stones had healing powers. One story says that an injured person should sit under the stones. Another person should pour water over the stones so that the water flows onto the injury. Then any injury would be healed. In about A.D. 1215 the poet Layamon wrote:

> The stones are great
> And magic power they have
> Men that are sick
> Fare to that stone
> And they wash that stone
> And with that water bathe away their sickness.[4]

Merlin and Stonehenge

Probably the most famous story of the origin of Stonehenge comes from the 12th century, a little earlier than Layamon's poem. It was written down by an early historian named Geoffrey of Monmouth. Geoffrey wrote that Stonehenge dated to the fifth century A.D. It was a little earlier than the time of the legend of King Arthur. The Angles and the Saxons were warriors who controlled parts of England and fought with the indigenous Britons. One fateful day the Saxons proposed to the British a peaceful meeting on the Salisbury Plain, and 460 British princes came to the meeting. At the peace council the treacherous Saxons were secretly armed with knives hidden in their boots. They attacked and killed every one of the unsuspecting princes. It was a tragedy and betrayal that the Britons could not forget. Arthur was not yet king. His uncle Ambrosius Aurelianus was the king, and he ruled with the help of Merlin the magician. The king visited the spot of the murders one day and decided that he wanted to erect a monument there to honor the fallen princes. But it had to be a special and unique memorial. Merlin knew of a memorial that would last forever. He said to the king, "Send for the Dance of the Giants that is in Killarus, a mountain in Ireland."[5] He explained that it was a circle of stones so large that no human could lift or move them. If the stones were placed in a circle on the Salisbury Plain, they would last forever.

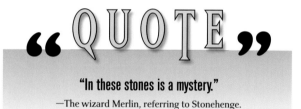

The king laughed and said it was preposterous. Ireland was too far away, and lifting and transporting the stones to England

King Arthur was linked to Stonehenge in legends. When he was a boy, he drew a special sword from out of a stone. No one but the true king of England could force the sword from the stone, but Arthur withdrew it easily, proving his destiny. One story says the sword had been made from a sarsen stone from Stonehenge.

would be a horrible job. Besides, England had plenty of its own stones. Merlin answered, "Laugh not so lightly. . . . In these stones is a mystery, and a healing virtue against many ailments. Giants of old did carry them from the furthest ends of Africa and did set them up in Ireland." He explained that the stones were worth any effort because they had the power to heal and were a product of witchcraft. So the king sent his brother Uther, who was the father of Arthur, to steal the Dance of the Giants and bring it back to England. Uther set out with an army of 15,000 men and a fleet of ships. Uther's army fought and defeated the Irish army that tried to stop them from stealing the treasure. But the British army was itself defeated by the circle of stones. No matter what they did, they could find no way to lift and haul the stones back to their ships. Then Merlin stepped in. He used his magic to make the stones as light as feathers so that Uther's army could carry them to their ships with ease. Geoffrey then says that the army "returned to Britain with joy." The men carried the stones to the Salisbury Plain, to the very spot of the slain princes' graves. There, they lifted the stones and "set them up about the compass of the burial-ground in such wise as they had stood upon mount Killarus."[6] And, thanks to Merlin, there they stand to this day.

King Arthur was linked to the Stonehenge legends, too. When he was a boy, he drew a special sword from out of a stone. No one but the true king of England could force the sword from the stone, but Arthur withdrew it easily, proving his destiny. One story says the sword had been made from a sarsen stone from Stonehenge. That was why it was magic.

If Not Merlin, Who?

For centuries, both before and after Geoffrey wrote his history of Stonehenge, people believed that Merlin was responsible for Stonehenge. They believed Stonehenge had been built in the fifth century and that it was a memorial and a burial ground for ancient British princes. Some historians suppose that Stonehenge got its name from this tale. They say that the word comes from *stan-hengist*, which means "uplifted stones." (Others say the name comes from the Saxon word *henge* and refers to "hanging stones,"

By the time of King Arthur and Merlin, Stonehenge was already more than 1,000 years old.

because the lintels seem to hang in the air.) Yet by the time of King Arthur and Merlin, Stonehenge was already more than 1,000 years old. People such as Geoffrey had no way of dating Stonehenge and so retold old tales to explain the presence of a monument that fascinated and perplexed them. As time passed, serious historians began to doubt Geoffrey's stories, but still they had only guesses about how Stonehenge came to be.

In the seventeenth century the great English architect Inigo Jones decided to solve the mystery of Stonehenge once and for all. He studied the monument, drew up plans that showed how the ruins must have looked when the monument was new, and theorized about who built it. His son-in-law wrote a book about Jones's findings. Jones tried to be scientific and logical. He said that the Merlin story was ridiculous. He explained that the Britons of prehistory could not have built Stonehenge, either, because they did not have the skill. He called them "savage and barbarous people . . . destitute of the Knowledge even to clothe themselves."[7] They were too primitive to have accomplished such a task as building Stonehenge. Jones concluded that the Romans must have built Stonehenge during the period from A.D. 43 to 410 when the Roman Empire occupied and ruled Britain. Only the Romans, who were highly civilized and skilled, had the ability to erect Stonehenge. Jones believed the site must have been a Roman temple. It honored the sky god, and that was why it had been built on an open plain. It was a place where animal sacrifices could be made to the god.

Tales for the Inexplicable

Jones's theory placed the age of Stonehenge earlier than the Merlin stories, but still it was not old enough. Other investigators chose the people of Denmark or druid priests from Gaul (now France) as the true builders of Stonehenge. Both peoples had invaded Britain before the time of the Roman occupation. If the Danes built it, it was a castle and magnificent throne for their king. For the druids it would have been a temple. These were both more ancient choices but still far too modern. It would be centuries more until the mystery of the age of Stonehenge would be solved.

As a matter of fact, the true builders of Stonehenge and its purpose seemed impossible to discover until the twentieth century. English diarist Samuel Pepys visited Stonehenge in 1668. He wrote in his diary, "God knows what their use was!"[8] As late as the nineteenth century, researchers continued to be baffled and to come up with strange theories about Stonehenge's origins. One English writer, Henry Browne, said, "Shall we . . . attribute their erection to Britons, to barbarians?—Silly thought!"[9]

Intensive Labor

Sarsen stone is extremely hard stone. It is three times harder than granite, so its shaping must have taken a very long time. Stonehenge expert Colin Burgess says that each tenon would have demanded the concentrated effort of 2 people for 1 month. Shaping each stone would have taken 50 people, working 10 hours a day, 7 days a week, for 2 years and 9 months.

He decided that the stones had been erected during the time of Adam and Eve and then partially destroyed by the great flood described in the Bible. In 1883 another writer, W.S. Blacket, said Stonehenge had been built by the lost people of Atlantis. He suggested that some of these people survived and moved to North America where they became Appalachian Indians, then traveled back to England and built Stonehenge.

Getting Beyond Fantasy

More careful historians concentrated on evidence and what they did not know. One historical journal editorialized in 1860 "that sober-minded people look on the solution as hopeless."[10] However, one nineteenth-century scientist believed discoveries about the age, meaning, and builders of Stonehenge were possible. He was W.M. Flinders Petrie. He did not find accurate answers, but he did have a plan. He said, "What is now necessary to settle this much-disputed subject is careful digging."[11] Digging is just what scientists, archeologists, and historians have done. Through careful exploration and analysis of their findings, they now know that the people who built Stonehenge were indeed those primitive barbarian Britons. And they were nowhere near as ignorant and incapable as modern people once thought.

CHAPTER 2

The People of Stonehenge

Stonehenge was a work in progress across a span of about 1,500 years and 70 or 80 generations of people. It went through at least 3 phases, built by peoples with evolving technologies, capabilities, and goals. Apparently, the people who erected Stonehenge got new ideas as time passed and elaborated on their epic monument. Stonehenge expert Rodney Castleden says the people were not at all ignorant or barbaric. They built a culture that lasted longer than any other, including the modern Industrial Age. Castleden sees the great stone structure as evidence of "the greatness of spirit and the depth of vision possessed by the Stonehenge people."[12]

More than 7,000 years ago the first farmers in the world began wandering into Britain when the last Ice Age was loosening its grip on the island. The homesteaders were New Stone

Age, or Neolithic, people. They no longer depended on hunting and gathering to eke out an existence and no longer lived in caves. They had learned agriculture and were able to lead a settled existence in permanent homes. By about 3000 B.C. they had developed a society that had the leisure to conceive the idea of Stonehenge. These people are referred to by some scientists as the Windmill people, because one of their first settlements was discovered in an area of Britain called Windmill Hill. It is from archeological digs at Windmill Hill and other sites that archeologists have learned about their lives.

Experts think the Windmill people lived in family groups or small clans of about 50 members. They built houses of wood or sod, perhaps with thatched roofs. They made tools and utensils of antlers, bones, and flint. They shaped pottery for household use, but they had no metal and apparently had not domesticated horses or invented the wheel. On the land they grew crops such as wheat and flax and raised cattle, sheep, goats, and pigs. Scientists know this because of seeds and bones found in the ruins of settlements. They have also discovered dog bones. Two kinds of dogs lived with the Windmill people—a large dog about the size of a Labrador retriever and a smaller one that was a kind of terrier. Some of these dogs were quite old when they died and so past being of practical use. This suggests that some dogs were pets and that working dogs were treated with affection.

Living Neolithic

These Neolithic people certainly did know how to clothe themselves. In settlement ruins and in graves their style of dress can be inferred from remains. They probably wore clothes of cured animal skins and leather and also knew how to weave linen from flax. Since they had domesticated sheep, they likely had woolen clothing, too. There are nowhere near as many sheep bones as cattle bones at cooking-hearth sites. This probably means the people slaughtered cattle most often for food and kept sheep for their wool. The flax seeds are another clue. Flax can be grown for the oil in the seeds, but scientists have also found small stones with drilled holes. These have been interpreted as parts of primitive looms for weaving cloth. Bone and antler pins that work best on leather clothes have been discovered, as well as hairpins, stone buttons, and belt fasteners.

Castleden believes that the people lived in a peaceful, friendly society, maintaining good relations with neighbors and operating on democratic principles. He says they may have had a headman or village elder, they may have had shamans or priests, but people were equal and followed their leaders out of respect. They had no central government and probably no war. Although many stone tools have been found, the people seem to have had few weapons. Their homes were not fortified for defense. They seem to have had enough food available to be relatively healthy and to have the spare time to make jewelry and other decorations, to plan feasts, and to bury their dead in elaborate graves.

Neolithic people, however, lived very short lives in comparison to modern people. The average life span was only about 30 to 40 years. Many children died in infancy. Only about 1 percent of the people lived past age 50. They did not get cancer or heart disease, but they sometimes had nutritional diseases such as rickets. Their teeth did not have cavities, but they were heavily worn down from eating rough grains and did get infections and abscesses. They had diseases such as polio, tuberculosis, and anthrax. They suffered many injuries, too, such as broken bones.

The most common problem for the New Stone Age people was

arthritis, and many developed painful arthritis at an early age. Castleden explains, "Some children as young as 6 developed osteo-arthritis in their spines, presumably as a result of carrying heavy loads. It comes as something of a shock to realise that the monuments were largely built by children."[13]

Stonehenge, Phase I

Children and young adults were probably the major builders of the first phase of Stonehenge. Although it was not the Stonehenge of today, it was still a huge creative endeavor. The people built the encircling bank, some 330 feet (100m) in diameter and 6 feet (1.8m) high. Inside the circle they dug the 56 evenly spaced holes, and outside the entrance they placed the Heel Stone. In the center of the great earthen circle, remnants of wood posts have been found. So some sort of wooden structure was built there, too. And that was Stonehenge, Phase I, in about 3000 B.C.

Scientists know which are the oldest parts of Stonehenge by using a method called radio-carbon dating. This is possible because of the cosmic rays from the sun that continually bombard the earth. These rays produce a radioactive form of carbon, called carbon 14. This carbon 14 is absorbed by plants that are eaten by animals. People eat the plants and animals, too, so every living thing has carbon 14 in its cells. When anything living dies, the carbon 14 starts to decay very slowly, and the radioactivity starts to disappear. Scientists can measure how much radioactivity is left in the remains of plant and animal tissues. This gives an estimate of age. Stones do not have carbon 14, but things like seeds, bones, and antlers do. This way of dating is not exact, but it can tell experts the age of anything that was alive within about 200 years.

The dirt and chalk of the ditch and banks cannot be carbon

The first stage of Stonehenge had two circular embankments separated by a ditch, Aubrey Holes, the Heel Stone, and some experts think a wooden structure in the middle.

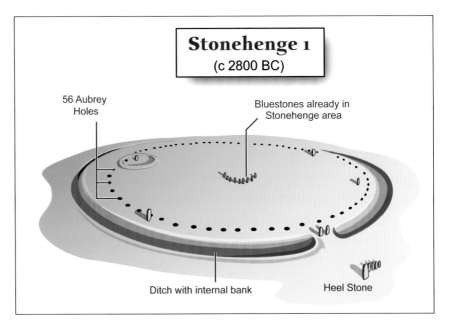

Stonehenge 1
(c 2800 BC)

56 Aubrey Holes

Bluestones already in Stonehenge area

Ditch with internal bank

Heel Stone

dated. Neither can the Heel Stone. However, at the bottom of the ditch archeologists discovered trash that the builders had thrown in, including meat bones, discarded antler picks, and shoulder blade shovels. These could be dated and gave scientists the answer to when Stonehenge I was constructed. The 56 holes yielded clues, too. These holes have been named the Aubrey Holes because it was John Aubrey who discovered them in 1665. In 1950 a burned piece of wood was discovered in one of the Aubrey Holes, and this wood identified the holes as part of the first phase of construction. Some of the Aubrey Holes contain human cremated remains, too, although exactly when they were buried is not certain.

No one truly knows what Stonehenge I meant to its Neolithic builders, but it must have taken decades and thousands of hours of labor. Obviously, it was a cooperative undertaking by people who put great value on its construction. It must have been a place of importance and meaning, and it was apparently used unchanged for some 450 years.

Stonehenge, Phase II

Then, sometime around 2600 B.C., the Beaker people began Phase II of Stonehenge construction. Stonehenge expert Christopher Chippindale says this was "the first of at least four remodellings of the original plan."[14] Perhaps these people were immigrants to Britain or perhaps they represented an evolving native society. Wherever they came from, they were people with new skills and improved technology. It was the beginning of the Bronze Age, a time when people discovered metals. At first they mined copper and gold, but then they learned to forge bronze from copper and tin, creating strong bronze tools, weapons, and decorations. It was a great leap forward

In 1665 John Aubrey discovered the Aubrey Holes. Some of the Aubrey Holes contain cremated human remains.

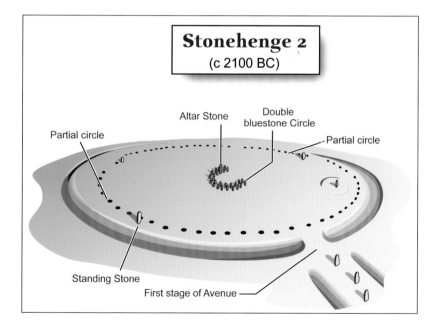

Stonehenge 2
(c 2100 BC)

Altar Stone
Double bluestone Circle
Partial circle
Partial circle
Standing Stone
First stage of Avenue

During the second phase of construction builders added two partial bluestone circles and several single standing stones to the structure.

for humanity. Pottery became more complex, too, and that is how the Beaker people came to be named. They invented a new pottery style that included drinking and water vessels called beakers.

The Beaker culture widened the Avenue, enlarged the entrance, and dug a protective trench around the Heel Stone. They transported 82 bluestones from the Prescelly Mountains and began to set them up in a double circle inside the banks and ditch. At some point, however, they seem to have decided not to complete the project. The bluestones were removed, and Stonehenge remained in this state until Phase III.

Stonehenge, Phase III

Later Bronze Age people known as the Wessex culture completed the Stonehenge that is known today. Their culture extended between about 2550 and 1600 B.C. These Stonehenge people were wealthy, powerful tradesmen and warriors. They were still people of prehistory—they had no written language. They did not build an ancient civilization as sophisticated as, for example, the ancient Egyptians. However, they had chieftains and kings, priests and soldiers, and probably a class of workers and farmers. They traded with other European peoples across the English Channel and perhaps raided them as well. They had metal tools and daggers, battle-axes, and rich gold adornments for their chiefs. The richest of them owned faience beads, which are blue glass beads from Egypt; bronze tools worked in Germany; and amber for jewelry from the Baltic.

When it came to building Stonehenge, these Wessex people were able to put forth a concerted effort, work together by the thousands, and accomplish an amazing task. Archeologist Colin Burgess says, "Stonehenge III was an undertaking on an almost unbelievable scale, even for a society as well-organized as we know existed

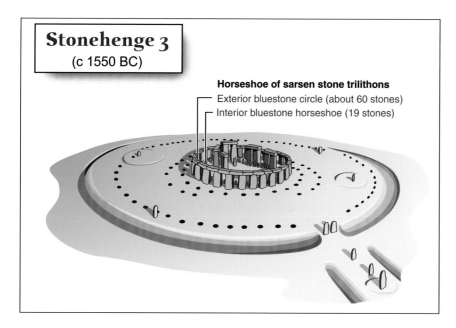

Stonehenge 3
(c 1550 BC)

Horseshoe of sarsen stone trilithons
— Exterior bluestone circle (about 60 stones)
— Interior bluestone horseshoe (19 stones)

During the third phase of construction builders added the complete circle of 30 standing stones capped by a continuous lintel of horizontal stones. In the center they built the horseshoe of trilithons.

in Wessex."[15] Although the Wessex culture was an agricultural one, the whole society was organized well enough to have strong leaders with a complex plan for building the megalithic monument. In years-long bursts of activity, the people completed Stonehenge.

Megabuilders

The sarsen stones for the megaliths and trilithons were hauled from their natural resting places on the Salisbury Plain about 24 miles (38.6km) to the north of Stonehenge. The stones were shaped and worked so that they would have smooth faces and would fit together with each other. The bluestones were hauled back in and arranged in the horseshoe shapes. Two more rings of deep holes were dug that today are labeled the Y and Z holes. The builders also erected the Altar Stone. Today it lies partially buried in the ground and is broken in two. Once, people believed the Altar Stone was a

Stonehenge Village

In 2007 archeologists discovered an ancient village at a site called Durrington Walls, about 2 miles (3.2km) away from Stonehenge. They speculate that the village was where the Stonehenge builders lived around 2600 B.C. So far, the diggers have unearthed about 100 house sites. Each house was about 16 feet (5m) square and made of wood with a clay floor and a hearth for cooking and heating. The archeologists found outlines of beds and cupboards. They discovered pig bones, stone tools, and pottery shards. There were so many half-eaten animal bones thrown on the floors that the scientists believe they have found signs of great feasts. Some say that perhaps this was not a permanent living place but a festival place for people visiting Stonehenge. The dig is not yet completed. Only eight house sites have been examined, and a detailed exploration of them all will take years. Professor Mike Parker Pearson, one of the leaders of the dig, is tremendously excited by the find. He says, "It is the richest—by that I mean the filthiest—site of this period

In 2007 archeologists discovered an ancient village at a site called Durrington Walls, about 2 miles away from Stonehenge. They believe the village was where the Stonehenge builders lived around 2600 B.C.

known in Britain. We've never seen such quantities of pottery and animal bones and flint."

BBC News, "Stonehenge Builders' Houses Found," January 30, 2007. http://news.bbc.co.uk.

place of human sacrifice, but scientists today do not think it ever was an altar. A hole nearby is probably where it once stood erect.

In 1953 Atkinson discovered that the Wessex people decorated some of the monoliths. They were adorned with chipped and carved outlines of a dagger and several ax heads. These carvings had been so eroded by weather that they were very faint, but they were there. Then in 1979 a scientist named Mike Pitts discovered that the Heel Stone had a mate, probably erected during this Phase III construction. Pitts found a matching hole with the stump of a stone still embedded within. So perhaps at this time the Heel Stone and its mate formed a kind of entrance gate.

How It Was Possible

Scientists have tried to estimate how much human labor all of this building took. The best guess is that Phase III Stonehenge took about 1.75 million hours of labor performed by thousands of people. The staggering amount of work required is hard to comprehend, but even harder to understand is how people with primitive tools, no oxen or horses for hauling, and no wheeled vehicles could accomplish such a task. Yet experts have shown how it could be done.

The sarsens were shaped and dressed with round stone mauls that could be held in the hands. Some were about the size of an orange and could be used for pounding. Others were as big as a basketball and probably were thrown at the sarsen slab. Geologist Edward H. Stone explains one shaping technique this way: "A number of men stand in line across the layer in the direction in which the slab is to be split. Each man has a maul which he holds between his two hands above his head. At a signal from the foreman each man dashes down his maul simultaneously on the [stone], which is thereby split across with a fairly even fracture."[16]

Moving the Stones

After the sarsen stones were shaped, they had to be hauled across the plain to the Stonehenge site. Some experts believe the stones were moved in winter by sliding them along the ice, wrapped with ropes and dragged by teams of people. Atkinson, however, thinks the stones were hauled onto a sledge by large teams of workers and dragged to Stonehenge little by little. A team of his students successfully did this in the 1950s with slabs of concrete that were the same size and weight as the sarsens. Other experts suggest the megaliths were moved on rollers. The rollers would have been logs that were continually moved in front by another work team as the stone was pulled forward. But Atkinson's students could not make that system work. The logs cracked on the rough ground of the Salisbury Plain.

Log rollers may have been used to get the bluestones part of the way from the Prescelly Mountains. Most experts believe these stones may have been hauled to the coast on sledges or rollers and then hoisted onto primitive dugout canoes that were lashed together. Then they could have been floated down the coast and up the Avon River to the Stonehenge site. This would have taken many years. By water it is 240 miles (386.2km) from the mountains to Stonehenge.

Raising the Stones

Once the megaliths were at Stonehenge, they had to be erected, and the lintels laid on top. Atkinson had an idea how this was done. First the workers would dig a deep pit with a kind of earthen ramp on one side. On log rollers the sarsen stone would be edged toward the ramp so that one end fell in the pit. Then, using a frame of wood and levers, the stone would be braced upward and hauled erect with ropes. Says scientist Gerald S. Hawkins,

And as soon as it was vertical, all empty space around its foot was filled, in an understandably frantic hurry. Anything and everything the laborers could reach they threw into the gaps to keep the stone from falling over: mauls and other tools, rocks, bones, scraps, turf—everything went in. The packing was then tamped hard. And then, probably, the standing monster was allowed to rest there for many months, so that its packing could harden and all settling cease.[7]

The monoliths were ready for the lintels. They could have been raised one at a time to the height of the sarsens on a platform of logs that completely surrounded each sarsen pair. Layers of logs would be added beside the first ones, and the lintel rocked slowly higher and higher on an ever upward-reaching platform of logs, perhaps only a foot at a time. Once at the height of the stone pair, the lintel would be pried and rolled into place with the mortise and tenon joint locked together. To raise even one lintel this way would have required about a mile (1.6km) of logs.

Able and Willing

All of this effort obviously was worth it to the Stonehenge people. During all the building phases, the work seems to have been done with enthusiasm. Experts do not believe any slave labor was ever involved as it was with the Egyptian pyramids. Stonehenge seems to have been a labor of love, yet carbon dates, construction methods, and ancient tools do not satisfactorily explain the motivation behind the work. Throughout England, however, there are clues. Stonehenge was not the only "henge." Stonehenge was once part of a whole culture of circles and rings that offer evidence today about the "why" of the monument.

CHAPTER 3

A Culture of Circles and Rings

In 1925 Royal Air Force pilot Gilbert Stuart Martin Insall was flying his World War I plane over Stonehenge and the Salisbury Plain. He was flying over a nearby newly plowed field when something odd caught his eye. Later he said that he saw markings in the field that seemed to be "a circle with white chalk marks in the center."[18] From his altitude he could look back and forth between the plowed field and Stonehenge 2 miles (3.2km) away. Somehow, they looked similar. He decided to keep his eye on the field. As the months passed, he repeated his flight and watched the field as the wheat grew. The green grain traced a picture of perfect crop marks. It grew dark green on the regular earth and lighter green in the chalky places. Insall could clearly see the pattern of a wide circular ditch with an opening, almost like Stonehenge's Avenue. Inside the circle he saw smaller round circles. They were the traces left by ancient postholes.

Insall had discovered another "henge." Henges are ovals or circles defined by earthen banks and ditches. Stonehenge is the most spectacular henge in Britain, but it is far from the only henge built by Neolithic and Bronze Age peoples. Archeologists have discovered more than 900 other ruins of ancient henges, and many are in and around the Salisbury Plain. Scientists theorize that the form was meaningful or sacred to Stonehenge peoples. They also assume that the henges could have had different purposes. They could have been meeting places, trading centers, holy sites, or even living spaces. Stonehenge was part of a greater cultural whole. By studying all the henges, the scientists get a better understanding of Stonehenge itself.

Woodhenge

The site discovered by Insall has been named Woodhenge. As its name implies, Woodhenge was not a stone circle; it was made of wood. There were 168 postholes arranged in concentric circles with a ditch and bank that was 279 feet (85m) in diameter. The wooden posts had been huge. Each weighed about 5 tons (4.5t) and stood about 25 feet (7.5m) tall. The posts no longer exist, and most of the site has been destroyed by generations of farming. But when archeologist Maud Cunnington led a dig of the ruins in 1928 and 1929, she found pottery that was made by the Beaker people and evidence of 2 more holes that may have held upright stones. She determined that the entrance to the henge faced the northeast and the midsummer sunrise, just as Stonehenge's entrance does. She also reported a gruesome discovery. Close to the center of the henge she found the grave of a child about three years old. Its skull had been split in half with an ax. In one part of the encircling ditch she found the remains of a teenager. Because of these finds,

Cunnington believed Woodhenge was a cemetery or a religious place of human sacrifice for the Beaker people. Carbon dating was not possible in the 1920s. Many experts decided Woodhenge was perhaps a huge, partially roofed or wood-domed structure where priests and holy persons lived and worked in 2500 B.C. For decades no one checked on this belief. No more digs were undertaken, and the child's skeleton was nowhere to be found. The remains were destroyed and lost during a World War II bombing of England.

In 2005 a second dig was begun at Woodhenge. It continues today and is being conducted by the Stonehenge Riverside Project. The Stonehenge Riverside Project is a team of archeologists, students, and other scientists from five major English universities. At Woodhenge the team found much older pottery than Beaker pottery and was able to date the oldest to about 3800 B.C. They also discovered that some of the wooden posts had been removed and replaced by standing stones that have now disappeared. In 2006 the team unearthed a small piece of bluestone. It was only 2 to 3 inches (5 to 7.6cm) long, but it had been chipped and worked with a stone tool. They also found evidence of burned sarsen pieces in some of the postholes. They found evidence of at least 3 stone buildings inside the henge, and they dug up animal bones that could have been discarded during feasts. No evidence of a child's grave was found in the center of Woodhenge. Now, although scientists do not know for sure what the finds mean, they question the use of Woodhenge as a temple. Lead archeologist Joshua Pollard thinks that Woodhenge was a place for the living, while Stonehenge may have been to honor the dead. He says, "The timber is associated with the living and may have been used for feasting or linked with the solstice whereas stone is connected with the ancestors."[19]

The team does not believe that there was a child sacrifice at Woodhenge either. What Cunnington found or how old the remains were will always remain a mystery. But archeology student Beatrice Greenfield says, "We've been able to wipe out a local myth about the grave."[20]

Other Henges

Although evidence of sacrifices is missing, both Woodhenge and Stonehenge seem to represent a holy shape that was used over and over in Neolithic culture. At Avebury, 17 miles (27.8km) from Stonehenge, is the ruin of the largest stone circle yet found in England. The ditch and bank are 1,101 feet (335.6m) in diameter, and they once enclosed a ring of 98 40-ton sarsen stones (36.4t). Almost all of these stones are gone now—probably broken and hauled away by later generations of people—but scientists can tell where they once stood. These sarsens, which date to around 3000 B.C., were not carved or shaped by the builders. They were just natural, rough stone slabs that were erected at Avebury. Some human bones have been found, so archeologists wonder if Avebury was a burial monument.

Stanton Drew, which is about 30 miles (48.3km) from Stonehenge, is a henge complex of three circles in stone. The largest, called the Great Circle, is the second largest henge in England. It is made up of natural, undressed sarsen stones, but scientists believe it was as complicated and elaborate as Stonehenge. It is 268 feet (112m) in diameter and was a circle of 27 stones. The other 2 stone circles are smaller. One was of 8 stones and the other of 12. There were 2 stone-lined entrances, too. The whole complex was twice as large as Stonehenge, but today most of the stones have disappeared.

Other Henges

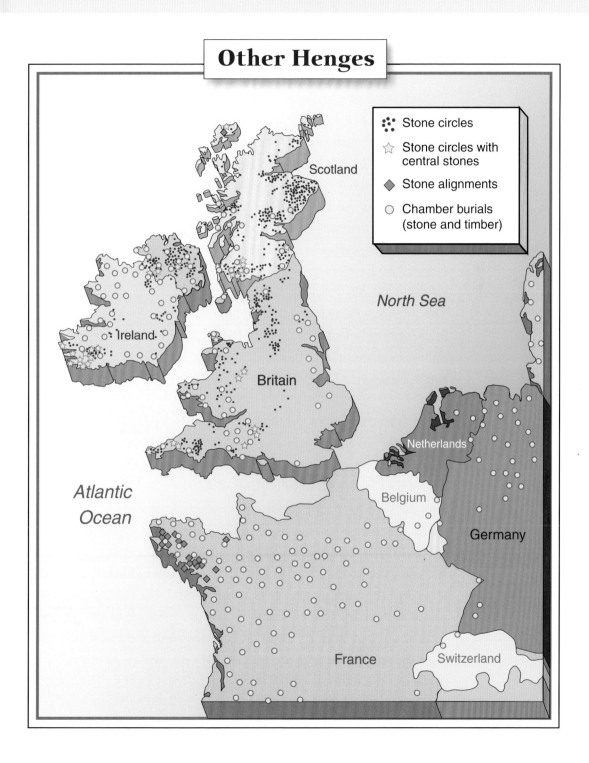

Legend:
- Stone circles
- Stone circles with central stones
- Stone alignments
- Chamber burials (stone and timber)

Scotland

North Sea

Ireland

Britain

Netherlands

Atlantic Ocean

Belgium

Germany

France

Switzerland

Archeologists date Stanton Drew to the Neolithic/Early Bronze Age era, but in 1997 an even older structure was discovered beneath the earth. Archeologist Geoffrey Wainwright led the digging team that led to the find. He said, "To our surprise and delight what emerged was a timber circle of about 3000 BC. There is now no timber left—it would have decayed long ago. But the disturbance of the soil when the pits were dug to take the uprights shows clearly."[21] Long buried underneath the stone circles, the henge seems to the archeologists to have been a great wooden temple. It was nine concentric circles of giant oak posts. The entrance to this ancient henge faced the northeast and the midsummer sunrise. Scientists believe the wooden henge probably lasted about 400 years until it began to decay and had to be replaced with stone circles.

The Marvelous Mound

The more archeologists explore the English countryside, the more henges they uncover, but henges are not the only circular structures of the Neolithic/Bronze Age era. Silbury Hill, for example, is the largest prehistoric man-made structure in Europe. As its name implies, it is a hill of huge dimensions. It is a 5.5-acre mound (2.2ha) of chalk and earth, 200 feet (61m) in diameter at its base, and 130 feet (39.6m) high. Scientists believe it was constructed about 2600 B.C. It is so large that Hawkins says, "One might call it the great pyramid of Europe."[22] Silbury Hill was originally built in 7 tiers, or terraces. Steps wound around it spiraling upward to the flat top of the cone shape. Today Silbury Hill is grassy and earth-covered, but once, at least part of the mound gleamed chalk-white in the sun.

The meaning and purpose of Silbury Hill are impossible to

know. It is not a tomb for a king as the pyramids were. No archeological digs have found any bones or human remains in its depths. It is another circle from the culture of the Stonehenge people for whom circles must have had special meaning. Castleden believes the circles represent the cycles of time and seasons and humanity's place in the eternal whole. There is no real beginning and no end, just like a circle. He says, "The Stonehenge people were intoxicated with their vision of the universe and their own place in it."[23] They built the circles to celebrate the vision. Castleden theorizes that the people saw Silbury Hill as a harvest monument—a religious place where a successful harvest could be celebrated and offerings made to the gods.

Barrows like Stonehenge?

People live in cycles, too. From birth to death is a kind of cycle if one is born from and returns to the world of the spirits. Is this why Stonehenge people were so "intoxicated" with the shapes of rings and circles? Some evidence for this idea can be found in the way the Stonehenge peoples buried their dead. The Neolithic people used long, earthen, communal mounds called barrows, but the builders of the megaliths buried their dead in round mounds. These burial mounds are clustered especially thickly around Stonehenge itself.

One of the most impressive long barrows is called West Kennet. It is not a circle, but it has an eerie resemblance to Stonehenge. It is an underground building with burial chambers that are constructed of upright sarsen stones with other sarsen stones supporting the roof that was covered with earth. The tomb is very large; it is 320 feet (100m) long and 8 feet (2.4m) high. Built about 3600 B.C., it was used for more than 1,000 years before the

Stonehenge people blocked off its entrance with more stones.

Burial chambers, however, take up only a small part of the space. No one knows the real reason for all the rest of the empty barrow, but Stonehenge expert Leon Stover believes that the whole mound was dedicated to ancestor worship and that it was like a church. The entrance to the barrow is marked out in a crescent shape called the forecourt. Many cooked cattle bones have been uncovered in the forecourt. Stover imagines, "Here the ancients held something like church socials, with something like barbecue roasts on the menu. . . . For 1,000 years the tomb was open for a succession of burials, the forecourt serving as a place for nothing short of ancestor worship." He adds that the later Stonehenge III people could have "got the idea for the monumental trilithons from the . . . entrances in chambered tombs like West Kennet."[24]

Circular Tombs

By the time of Stonehenge III, long barrows were replaced by individual round burial mounds. Almost 350 of them are found around Stonehenge. Many of these graves have been robbed or destroyed over the years, but some have been found intact. The grave remains may be cremated, but in other instances they are buried in a fetal position, curled up like a fetus in the womb. Buried with the remains are different sorts of grave offerings. Some have beakers; others have daggers, tools, or jewelry. Many have what are called pygmy cups. They are tiny round cups that do not seem to have a practical use. They are too small for drinking cups and often have holes bored in them anyway. They may be another circular symbol used by the Stonehenge people.

The Meaning of Circles

All these clues suggest that circles and rings are representative of a culture that uses sacred symbols to express their relationship with nature. Castleden says that the Stonehenge people were obsessed with death, but this obsession was not morbid. He calls the circles and ceremonies a "dialogue with death" that concentrated on the cycle of birth, death, and rebirth. Castleden thinks that is what the circles represent; that they speak of the human cycle and also of nature's fertility cycle of seasons and renewal: Winter is like death; spring is a birth; and harvest time is the rich, fertile season that all farmers depend on for life itself. He says the long barrows "were not monuments to the dead, but to Death itself, and they should be seen as magic gateways through which life could be started anew and where the living and the dead could meet."[25]

If Castleden is right, the trilithons of Stonehenge may also represent magic gateways to the afterlife. All the circular structures may have this kind of mystical meaning. Archeologist Terence Meaden speculates that the Stonehenge people worshipped a great Earth Mother. He explains, "The Goddess was universal. Soil and earth were her body. Just as life issues forth at birth so is life reclaimed at death, for Earth is both womb and grave, at once fertile and protective." Meaden says that "entering the grave . . . was like returning to the womb."[26] He believes that religion and the Earth Mother explain all the circles and rings of the Stonehenge people: The structures stand for the people's belief in the goodness of the Earth Mother, the richness of the Earth, and the promise of eternal life.

The circles in the earth represent the Earth Mother, but Meaden also believes that the standing stones and pillars built by the Wessex culture mean something else. They reach for the sky and maybe to a different kind of god—a male Sky God. He calls this a "Sacred Marriage" of the Earth Mother and the Sky God. He says, "Not only did this concept glorify the Goddess to an exceptional degree, but it embraced, to a lesser extent, her marriage partner the Sky God as well."[27] Within their sacred circles, Meaden believes, the Stonehenge people were protected by their gods, expressed their connection with nature and the afterlife, and were one with the great cycle of life.

The people who built henges and rings left no description of themselves or their religion. Experts have no history of them except the ruins of their buildings and their tombs. Certainly the burials strongly suggest that they believed in an afterlife and had a religion, but no one can be sure what that religion was. The rings and circles of the tombs are so similar to the henges that religion can be inferred but not proved. Since henges were unique to the Stonehenge people, scientists cannot even compare the structures to those of other ancient peoples who did leave better records of themselves. However, scientists do know that people elsewhere in Europe worshipped the Earth Mother. Idols of her have been found in their graves and in caves where people lived. Evidence has been found of a Sky God, too, but whether the Stonehenge people had the same beliefs cannot be known for sure. All scientists really know is that rings and circles were very important to the Stonehenge people. Most experts do believe that they are religious in nature, just because they were apparently so important. Many also believe that structures such as Stonehenge may have had more than one meaning. They may

Lines Among the Circles

One structure of the Stonehenge people was not a circle. It was an earth line or a kind of path called a cursus. A cursus runs beside Stonehenge that is a straight line 100 yards (91m) wide and 1.75 miles (2.8km) long. It is defined by a low bank and narrow ditch on either side. The largest cursus built by Stonehenge people is 302 feet (92m) wide and 6.5 miles (10.5km) long. Many of these earth lines have been found, but no one has any idea what they were for. Guesses run from lunar sighting lines to processional pathways for rituals to race courses for athletes. Most are faint and hardly visible today. They are just one more mystery in the many mysteries of the Stonehenge people.

have represented both life and death. They may have been both practical and sacred.

Someone's Religion

Modern explorers can use carbon dating, archeological digs, and the evidence from other cultures to try to understand the Stonehenge people, but in the past these tools were not available. The Stonehenge builders were misinterpreted and misunderstood for many years. Even in the 1950s, Atkinson, who did think Stonehenge was a temple, thought the Stonehenge people were barbarians and too primitive to have had a rich culture. Atkinson knew that Stonehenge dated from the Bronze Age, but for centuries other experts did not. Nevertheless, the monument itself felt awe-inspiring and sacred, and an explanation was needed. So, Stonehenge became associated with another mystical people who had nothing to do with its construction. Today, people who consider themselves the spiritual descendents of those other people still claim Stonehenge as their own.

CHAPTER 4

Celts and Stonehenge

On the night of June 20, 2007, about 24,000 people gathered at Stonehenge to await the summer solstice sunrise on June 21. They were all there to celebrate the longest day of the year. Hare Krishnas drummed, clapped, and danced. New Age Wiccans—modern pagan witches—chanted. Jugglers performed, gypsy fiddlers played their instruments, and festive visitors showed off their fancy hats or waved colorful ribbons. Many people drank and partied boisterously. In the midst of the revelry roamed New Age Celtic priests. Some were dressed in antlers and oak leaves. Others wore black or white robes. They were there to conduct a sacred ceremony to welcome the sun and celebrate the spiritual union of Earth and the sun, as they do at Stonehenge every summer. Each winter they do the same during the winter solstice—the shortest day of the year when the sun shines for the fewest hours.

People of many faiths and beliefs gather at Stonehenge for the summer solstice each year. In 2007, 24,000 people gathered to watch the sunrise.

The Celtic priests are New Age druids who try to reenact the religious ceremonies of the ancient druids and connect with their Celtic ancestors. They feel a special relationship with Stonehenge. Druid priest David Loxley says, "Stonehenge is like mother earth communicating with the Sun."[28] Despite a drizzle of rain, people kept a vigil throughout the night. As dawn approached, thick clouds obscured the sunrise, but the followers of druidism and their priests were the center of attention.

The priests had placed symbols of the four elements of earth, fire, water, and air around Stonehenge. As dawn came close, they collected these symbols and brought them to the Stone of Sacrifice. They said prayers to express their respect for Mother Earth and to give thanks for the miracle of life. They bowed to the sacred marriage between the powerful sun and the nurturing Earth. As the druids stood in a sacred circle and chanted, the sun rose. Unlike in past years, no one could see the moment it seemed to hang almost directly over the Heel Stone. All they could see was a rosy, red glow in the east. Nevertheless, the worshippers felt joy and gave praise to the living stones that welcomed the sun. Another cycle of seasons had begun. The modern-day druids believed they had used holy Stonehenge as the ancients meant for it to be used. The festival was over for another year.

Connecting Celts to Stonehenge

The Celts did not build Stonehenge, but for decades New Age followers of the pagan religion called druidism have claimed Stonehenge as their own temple. Druidism was the religion of the ancient Celts, and the druids were their priests. For centuries people connected Stonehenge with the Celts and believed it was a druid temple. The idea of Stonehenge as druidic started with John Aubrey in the seventeenth century. When he explored Stonehenge and found the Aubrey Holes, he also concluded that the monument was much older than the Roman era. He decided that the druids, a more ancient people, had directed the building of Stonehenge. By Aubrey's time these druids were legendary and much admired as a wise and knowledgeable lost race. They seemed a logical choice as the builders of Stonehenge.

There really were Celts in ancient Britain. They immigrated to Britain from Gaul around 500 B.C. and apparently were a powerful influence on ancient British culture. By their time, Stonehenge had been long abandoned by its builders, and whether the Celts used Stonehenge is unknown. Much knowledge of the druid religion is lost in the mists of time. Although the culture did know

and use Greek and Roman writing, most of its traditions were passed down orally. No one today truly knows the details of their prayers or their way of life, but some information about them was written down by their Roman conquerors in the first century. Since the Romans despised the Celts and their religion, perhaps some of the information is biased.

Stalking the Real Celts

Julius Caesar wrote that druidism originated in Britain. He said that the Celts were divided into three classes of people—the knights or warriors, the high priests or druids, and the rest of the people who were "treated almost as slaves." He described the druids as wise and powerful but also as cruel practitioners of human sacrifice. In his book *The Gallic Wars* he wrote,

> "Report says that in schools of the druids they learn by heart a great number of verses, and therefore some persons remain twenty years under training . . . the cardinal doctrine which they seek to teach is that souls do not die, but after death pass from one to another . . . besides this, they have many discussions as touching the stars and their movement, the size of the universe and of the earth."

He went on to describe a terrible sacrifice to the gods in which the druids built "figures of immense size, whose limbs, woven out of twigs, they fill with living men and set on fire, and the men perish in a sheet of flame."[29]

The Celts, led by their druids, believed in a polytheistic religion, one of many gods of earth, sky, trees, and rivers. The druids

The Romans were appalled by druidic practices, especially the practice of human sacrifice. When they conquered Britain, they brutally attempted to wipe out the Celtic religion. Here, in an artist's vision, Roman soldiers attempt to stop a sacrifice at Stonehenge.

performed ceremonies to keep the gods happy, communicated with the gods and acted as judges and wise men for the people. They were brilliant teachers and religious philosophers. They studied the stars and the heavens and were said to be able to read omens and predict eclipses. They taught the sons of the Celtic kings. They were believed to possess magical knowledge and healing abilities. Pliny, another Roman historian, explained that oak trees and mistletoe were sacred to the druids and were used in magic ceremonies to heal sickness, but he also said that the druid magicians did evil things. He described human sacrifices and then eating human flesh for healing some sicknesses.

The Romans were appalled by druidic practices and probably worried about the power that druid priests wielded. When they conquered Britain, they brutally attempted to wipe out the Celtic religion. They killed many druid priests and forced other believers into hiding. Then Christianity came to Britain in about A.D. 300, and druidism gradually disappeared as a culture and a religion. When later generations remembered the religion, they talked about mystic and magical power, not evil behavior. Perhaps the druids indulged in human sacrifice and ritual cannibalism, but historians after the Roman era did not describe cruelty. Maybe, say experts, the druid religion evolved and became kinder or maybe the Romans exaggerated for propaganda purposes. Whatever the truth, by the time of Aubrey, Celts and druids were considered highly civilized and talented ancient people.

Romantic Celts

Aubrey's declaration that Stonehenge was a druid temple captured the imagination of William Stukeley, a historian in the eighteenth century who greatly admired the druids. He studied Stonehenge and other ancient circles and came to the conclusion that Stonehenge was a "noble work" by an ancient race so learned and holy that it should "make our moderns ashamed."

Stukeley was supposed to be a scientist, but he made up many tales about the druids at Stonehenge, including the idea that they had worshipped serpents. He called Stonehenge a "serpent temple,"[30] and he drew pictures of saintly looking druids at peace with nature. He was also the first researcher to notice that the position of the Heel Stone marked the midsummer solstice and to suppose that Stonehenge was a kind of giant druidic calendar of the heavens. For many people this discovery just proved how wonderfully capable the ancient druids were.

During the 18th and 19th centuries all things druidic were romantically admired, and the Celtic link to Stonehenge grew and grew. Minister William Cooke wrote that the Stonehenge people gave 1/10 of their income to support the druid temple, just as Christians tithed to their churches. He compared Stonehenge to the altar that Moses built and supposed that the circle represented God and the Holy Trinity. Popular opinion was that Stonehenge was a monument to be proud of because British druidic heritage was so admirable. Poets and men of letters perpetuated the druidic myth. Poet and essayist Dr. Samuel Johnson, who also wrote a famous early English dictionary, believed Stonehenge was built by the ancient druids. In one of his poems John Keats sang "Of Druid stones, upon a forlorn moor."[31] Lord Byron linked Stonehenge with the druids in his poem "Don Juan." William Wordsworth wrote of the druid builders of Stonehenge as the "barbaric" visionaries in "Our dim ancestral Past."[32]

The poet and artist William Blake romantically linked Stonehenge not only with druids but with Christianity. He looked on druidism as the beginning of all true religion and supposed that Christ had visited ancient Britain and been taught by philosopher druids. He believed ancient Britain was the original "Jerusalem"—

the Holy Land. He referred to Stonehenge as the place "where Jerusalem's foundations began" and wrote, "Thence stony Druid Temples overspread the island white thence . . . through the whole Earth were rear'd."[33] Blake, who was a druid, was sure that Christ was also a druid. He believed it was logical and meaningful to be a Christian and a druid at the same time. Druidism became for many the religion of a mythical golden age when people were one with nature and all was peace and love.

New Age Druids

In 1781 a new order of druids was established in London, and Blake was one of its leaders, or archdruids. The group was named "The

William Wordsworth, pictured, felt the druids were the visionaries of the long lost past.

Most Ancient Order of Druids" and sought to rediscover and revive ancient druidic beliefs and practices. One of its original founders was Henry Hurle of London, who greatly admired the druids. In 1771 he suggested, "My proposition is that we form a society for social feeling and we assume the title of those learned men (The Druids), and that we will adopt the endearing name of brothers universally amongst us."[34] This society was begun 10 years later and is still active today. Since it was established, about 300 other groups of people around the world have embraced druidism and become New Age druids. Many of these people say that druidism is not a religion but a philosophy and a way of thinking. They say they are pagans who believe in the spirits of places, living things,

Nature's Mystic Circles

Some of the largest and oldest mushroom colonies on Earth grow around Stonehenge. These circles of mushrooms are called fairy rings. Stonehenge's fairy rings are so huge that they can best be seen from high overhead in an airplane. Some can actually be seen from satellites. (Fairy rings got their name from folklore, which says they are where fairies and pixies hold midnight dances.)

and elements; that stone circles have spirits; trees have spirits; and the whole of life is a web of spirituality. They also believe in reincarnation.

Philip Carr-Gomm is a member of "The Order of Bards, Ovates, and Druids" (OBOD). He explains that bards are the "keepers of tradition" in druidism. They are the storytellers and poets. An ovate is a prophet and healer who studies natural herbal healing. He or she also leads a festival to celebrate death but believes it is really a celebration of the next stage of life. Carr-Gomm says ovates consider death as a path from "one way of being to [being] reborn to a deeper experience of being alive." Druids, he says, are the wise philosophers, teachers, advisers, and judges—the authorities "in matters of worship and ceremony."[35]

Carr-Gomm explains that different druid groups may have different beliefs. They may believe, for example, in many gods and goddesses or in one God or only in the spirits in earthly things. But, he says, "druids share a belief in the fundamentally spiritual nature of life." All druids revere nature, and, Carr-Gomm adds, "druids love stones and stone circles."[36] He and other druidic followers believe that Stonehenge is a very sacred place. For at least 100 years, the modern druids have claimed Stonehenge as their own.

New Druids and Stonehenge

No one is exactly sure when modern druids began to celebrate festivals and ceremonies at Stonehenge. However, druids did hold an elaborate ceremony there in 1905. They inducted 300 new priests into their religion in the middle of the megaliths. Ever since then, modern druids continue to journey to Stonehenge for the summer and winter solstices. They try to recreate ancient ceremonies there and celebrate their oneness with nature and its changing seasons.

For several years it was easy for the druids to enter Stonehenge. It lay on private property and was not protected in any way. In 1915 it was given to the British government, and it was designated a national monument in 1919. Stonehenge was protected from harm and fenced off so that most people could not get inside. Druids, however, are allowed to enter the monument for the summer and winter festivals. The sunrise over the Heel Stone is celebrated at the summer solstice and the sunset over the Heel Stone is celebrated at the winter solstice. The druids say they have a right to be there, even though scientists say that druids had nothing to do with the building of Stonehenge.

Some historians do believe that the druids could have used Stonehenge even though they did not build it. No proof has ever been found for this idea, but once Stonehenge was abandoned, the druids may have used it for a temple. Stover says that "during the Roman occupation . . . the site may still have been active as a magic place of Druidic resistance."[37] Stover and some New Age druids also surmise that the people of the Wessex culture were "proto-Celts," meaning that they were the forerunners of the Celts, not a completely different culture. The idea is that Celts did not immigrate in huge numbers to Britain and then wipe out the Wessex culture. Instead, the Wessex culture slowly evolved into a Celtic one.

If the proto-Celts idea is true, then perhaps there is a druid connection to Stonehenge. Just a few druids from Europe could have influenced the Wessex people and helped to change the culture. Stover says, "It is altogether reasonable to suppose that protodruids planned the building of Stonehenge."[38] Protodruids are the priests and priestesses of a religion that grew into druidism. Experts such as Stover see the ancient religions of Earth Mother and Sky God as growing and changing over time. They believe that the Wessex priests and healers who built sacred circles are the ancestors of the druids.

Carr-Gomm believes Stover is correct. He explains:

> Although the Druids have always been associated in the popular imagination with stone circles such as Stonehenge, academics until recently dismissed this idea. Historians used to say that the Druids couldn't have used Stonehenge and all the other stone circles in Britain, because the Druids

were the priests of the Celts, and the Celts only arrived in Britain in 500 BCE. Since no stone monuments were built after 1400 BCE, they pointed to the gap of nine hundred years separating the last of the stone circles from the arrival of the Druids. But . . . many historians [have] changed their minds. They realized that the origin of the so-called Celtic tribes was far more complex than originally presumed, and suggested instead that early or Proto-Celts were probably in Britain as early as 2000 BCE—when the great stone monuments were still being built—and that they could well have been involved in their use or construction.[39]

True or False?

Not everyone agrees that protodruids were Stonehenge people. Most scientists say that the druid culture is nowhere near old enough to have been involved in the building of Stonehenge. Many experts say a true Celtic migration did not occur in Britain until about 500 B.C. They call the New Age druids "mock druids." They insist that Stonehenge was not a druid temple. Hawkins says today's druids are conducting "unauthentic ceremonies" at Stonehenge. He adds, "It is a pity, because this carrying-out of made-up 'rituals' by a group which has no real knowledge of what ancient druids thought or did—and no proof that they existed when Stonehenge was new—only confuses the ignorant and annoys the serious students of the past."[40]

The serious students of the past are not even sure whether Stonehenge was a temple at all. Mystery still surrounds Stonehenge and its builders. Experts say they know who built Stonehenge. They probably have solved the mystery of its construction, too. But no one can answer with certainty why Stonehenge was built. This is the question that occupies the scientists and experts who study Stonehenge today, and they have many theories about the original intent of the Stonehenge peoples.

CHAPTER 5

Exploring the "Why" of Stonehenge

Stonehenge is unique among the ruins in England because of the size and shape of the megaliths, because of the trilithons, and because its purpose is so unclear. It seems obvious to experts, though, that it must have been a very special place. Investigators link the evidence found at Stonehenge and other ruins, put the pieces of evidence together, and try to come up with logical theories about what moved the Stonehenge peoples to construct their unique monument. Since Stonehenge was an evolving structure over a period of at least 1,000 years, the investigation is not easy. Modern scientists and historians have developed several major theories about the "why" of Stonehenge.

It Was a Fortress

One of the earliest theories about Stonehenge is that it was built as a fortress, a place where associated family groups and tribes

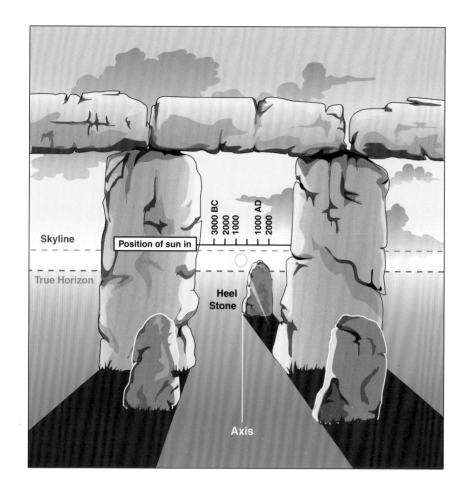

Skyline

Position of sun in

3000 BC
2000
1000
1000 AD
2000

True Horizon

Heel
Stone

Axis

This diagram shows the Heel Stone and its alignment with the sun.

could find protection from the raids of neighboring enemies or from invading warriors from across the English Channel. This theory assumes that the Wessex people were from a warlike, aggressive culture. Scientists are no longer sure that the Wessex culture was a warrior culture, and most now doubt that Stonehenge was a place of shelter and defense. Few signs of human habitation exist around Stonehenge. If people occupied it, even periodically, archeologists should be able to find meal leftovers such as animal bones. They should find evidence of tools, charred wood bits from cooking fires, and other discarded trash. Very few such remains have been found at Stonehenge. Weapons have not been found in the earth at Stonehenge either. It seems only logical that battle-axes and broken spears would be left from wars, but they are nowhere to be found.

Stonehenge itself does not seem to be suited for a defensive shelter. The circle of stones, say most experts, could not have supported a roof. These experts point to the differing heights of the megaliths and the trilithons. It is hard to imagine how a roof of thatch or wood could have been supported. Also, without a center pole, the center of the roof would have had to be left open. Perhaps added wooden posts could have supported a roof, but archeological digs have not uncovered any evidence of such posts.

The most important evidence that Stonehenge was not a fort rests on the placements of the bank and ditch. Ancient people did use a bank and ditch system to slow invaders and make them vulnerable to a counterattack. But this kind of defensive system depended on a large bank or banks placed outside the encircling ditch. As warriors climbed over the banks, they found themselves in a ditch where they could be trapped when the fort's inhabitants launched an assault. Stonehenge's bigger bank is inside the ditch. This would not seem to have any protective effect. Few experts today believe that Stonehenge was a place to live in or a protective enclosure.

Yet Stonehenge does seem to resemble the roundhouses, circular meeting places, and tombs of the Neolithic/Bronze Age people. Castleden believes that the shape of Stonehenge is a symbol. He says Stonehenge "was the image of home" and a "nostalgic and sentimental image"[41] of ancestors long departed and the houses they inhabited. In other words, the living were linked to the dead by the circles of stone. The question of purpose cannot be answered with "fortress" or "dwelling place" agrees Meaden. "The answer lies with religion."[42]

It Was the Sun God's Altar

Many Stonehenge experts see the monument as a temple, but what kind and how was it used? Experts have attempted a his-

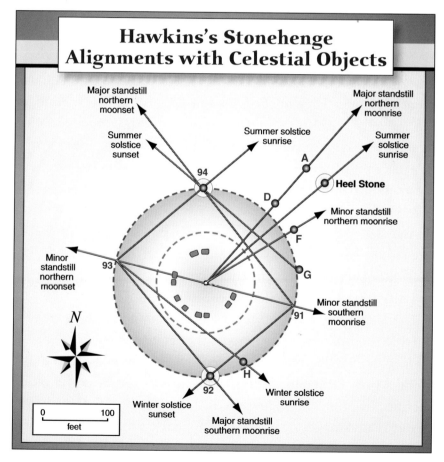

Hawkins's Stonehenge Alignments with Celestial Objects

Major standstill northern moonset

Major standstill northern moonrise

Summer solstice sunset

Summer solstice sunrise

Summer solstice sunrise

94

A

D

Heel Stone

Minor standstill northern moonrise

F

Minor standstill northern moonset

93

G

91

Minor standstill southern moonrise

N

H

92

Winter solstice sunset

Winter solstice sunrise

0   100
feet

Major standstill southern moonrise

Scientist Gerald Hawkins charted 165 important correlations between Stonehenge stones and holes and events in the sky depending on the time of year.

torical reconstruction of Stonehenge to answer these questions. Some experts speculate that it was a sacred place where the few holy priests and shamans conducted secret ceremonies. It was dedicated to sun worship. The priests and magicians were able to awe the common people with their magic and arcane knowledge by using the sunrise and sunset over the Heel Stone to predict the seasons, to tell the people when to plant crops, and perhaps by bidding the sun to return for another year. For a people dependent on crops and agriculture for survival, this would have been powerful magic indeed. Rituals to persuade the sun to return may have included human sacrifice, according to this theory.

If the priests needed to know when the summer solstice occurred, however, they needed only two stones, not a giant monument of stones. They needed to sight toward the Heel Stone by placing only one other stone in a line toward the summer solstice sunrise. The same argument might hold for rejecting Stonehenge as a place only for the chosen few. Stonehenge is large enough for a crowd of people. Such a large monument was not needed for just a few priests and their secret rituals. Nowadays, scientists do not believe that Stonehenge people practiced human sacrifice either. This belief may have started with the idea that druids built Stonehenge and is probably responsible for the names of the Altar Stone and the Slaughter Stone.

The Slaughter Stone lies mostly buried in the earth today, just outside the main henge. The part that is visible has scallops on its face, and little holes dot one end. It is covered with reddish streaks that earlier historians thought was the dried blood of sacrificial victims. Investigation of this stone proves that theory wrong. Hawkins says the scallops appear on many other sarsen stones. He adds, "The little holes were dug in modern times, by some enterprising person wishing to split off a piece of the huge stone."[43] The reddish streaks are not blood, human or otherwise. They are streaks of iron ore running through the sarsen. Finally, archeologists learned long ago that the Slaughter Stone originally stood upright. It was one of two stones marking the entrance to Stonehenge. In 1919 archeologist Colonel William Hawley conducted a dig at Stonehenge. Under the Slaughter Stone he found a hole in the chalky earth. In the hole was a broken piece of sarsen. Hawley thus provided the first evidence that the stone had stood erect in the time of the Stonehenge people. And no evidence of human sacrifice has ever been found in or around Stonehenge.

Jones misnamed the fallen Altar Stone in the seventeenth century. It probably once stood upright in the center of the monument. The original hole in which it was placed is assumed to be hidden under the fallen slab. It did not lie flat as Jones saw it, but it is a unique stone at Stonehenge. It is the only one with greenish mica glittering in its sandstone. It was not an altar slab; it was not part of a temple of sacrifice, but, asks Meaden, "Why should this particular type of stone, from so far away, have been selected for the focal position of the Neolithic masterwork?"[44]

It Was a Fertility Temple

Meaden's answer is a different sort of religious monument. He puts together all the evidence from the Stonehenge people with the traditional beliefs of other primitive agricultural societies, both ancient and modern. The belief in a supreme Earth Mother is a common thread that he applies to Stonehenge's construction. He concludes that Stonehenge is a sacred circle, and that like all the Neolithic sacred circles, it represents a creation myth: It was a temple, a womb that mimicked caves and entrances to the womb of the great Earth Mother herself; Stonehenge is a womb; and the Altar stone is in reality the Goddess Stone, the most important part of the yearly ceremony that took place at Stonehenge for all its believers. Meaden also says that the Heel Stone was erected so as to create an "eclipse trick"[45] with a deep meaning. As the sun, or Sky God, rose in midsummer, it was at first very low on the horizon. When the full orb was above the horizon, it moved in its path such that, from inside Stonehenge, it disappeared be-

Bluestone Controversy

Although most scientists believe Stonehenge's bluestones were brought to the Salisbury Plain by the builders, a few disagree. Stonehenge expert Aubrey Burl believes that the bluestones were not transported from the Prescelly Mountains by the Stonehenge people. Instead, they were moved by Ice Age glaciers to the Salisbury Plain. The Stonehenge people found them there and used them in building the monument.

In 2006 a scientific team from Open University in Britain chemically analyzed different bluestone axes

hind the Heel Stone for a few minutes. The shadow created by this event touched and lengthened across the Goddess stone. The mica in the stone glowed reddish as the sun touched it and then dimmed as the shadow climbed the face of the stone. According to Meaden, people did not watch the sun rising over the Heel Stone. They stood with their backs to it, facing the Goddess Stone, and watched the shadow touch its surface.

Meaden says the shadow on the Goddess stone represented a

to see where they came from. Bluestone axes in England are not chemically the same as bluestone axes in Wales, and the English axes are chemically similar to Stonehenge's stones. This evidence supports the glacier theory. However, there are no bluestones littering the Salisbury Plain now, say other experts, so does that mean the glacier brought just enough bluestones for the Bronze Age people to use them all? Others insist that the last Ice Age did not move any glaciers as far south as the Salisbury Plain. No one knows which theory is true since there is evidence to support both sides of the argument.

symbolic mating of the gods. It was fertility worship. The wedding "provided a rational explanation for the periodical renewal of the world and the harmonious cycle of life, death, and rebirth." Stonehenge was the center of the universe and the place to reenact the mating of the Great Goddess with the Sky God, when the sun was at its most powerful. Meaden explains, "Stonehenge was a replica of the universe in microcosm. The midsummer marriage was a repetition of the Creation in an intelligible, memorable, and inspiring form."[46] Stonehenge was not a secret place for the chosen few, although no doubt the priests performed the ceremonies and said the prayers, says Meaden. It was a gathering place where all the people could celebrate Earth's continuing renewal and give thanks for the fertility of Earth.

It Was an Ancient Computer

Meaden's interpretation of Stonehenge can neither be proved nor disproved, but it represents a generally accepted theory that Stonehenge was a religious place, ruled over by priests and shamans, where large groups of people came together for worship, feasting, and celebration. Another theory suggests a more ambitious purpose. According to this idea, Stonehenge was actually an ancient astronomical observatory. Hawkins was the first modern scientist to suggest that Stonehenge was a kind of primitive computer with which the priests could develop an accurate calendar and predict important solar and lunar events. Hawkins was the first archaeoastronomer. Archaeoastronomy is the study of the astronomical beliefs and practices of the ancient world. It is a way of understanding how Stonehenge people may have understood the universe and Earth's place in it.

The sky can be viewed as a giant dome or bowl inverted over

the seemingly flat landscape of Earth. On the "face" of this bowl are all the heavenly bodies—stars, planets, sun, and moon. The positions of these bodies can be measured by sighting from markers such as stones or gateways placed on the ground. The positions are measured in degrees, just as mathematicians measure a circle (or half-circle). Star groups rotate slowly in unison across the bowl. The sun and moon move from east to west in an arc across the bowl, but as the year progresses, the path of the arc is different. Where the sun rises and sets is different, too. In summer, for example, the sun's path is high in the sky. During the winter it is lower. It does not rise directly in the east and set exactly in the west during most of the year either. This happens on only two days in the year, called the autumn and spring equinoxes.

Earth's axis is tilted, which causes different seasons. This tilt, however, slowly changes over thousands of years. So the tilt was not exactly the same for Stonehenge people as it is for modern British people. The actual angle on the bowl where the sun rises is slightly different, both during a year and over time. Hawkins explains, "The sun swings annually . . . from +23.5 degrees (north) [to] -23.5 degrees (south)."[47] In Britain the sun moves from north to south as summer progresses to winter. Then it seems to move back again, from south to north as the summer solstice approaches. This movement means that the sun rises in the northeast at Stonehenge on the longest day of the year.

This is what Hawkins assumes is the purpose of the Heel Stone as viewed from the center of Stonehenge. It points to the northeast rising of the sun on the summer solstice. But, say some scientists, it does not point to the sunrise with accuracy. Actually, the Heel Stone, even if it was standing erect, does not line up exactly with the summer solstice sunrise today. It begins a little to the left of the Heel Stone and passes a bit to the stone's right as it rises. Mistakenly, some scientists in the past thought this was due to the tilt change in Earth's axis, but the tilt does not account for the "error." Even when Stonehenge was new, the sun never rose exactly over the Heel Stone. This is a major criticism by some experts of the whole idea of Stonehenge as an observatory. It is one reason Meaden argues that the shadow, not the sunrise, was the most important.

Many Victorian novelists made Stonehenge the setting for tragic deaths or God's retribution for sins and immorality. In 1891 Thomas Hardy used Stonehenge in his novel Tess of the D' Urbervilles.

Eclipses, Equinoxes, and Solstices

Hawkins, however, believes that the Heel Stone was only one marker in the Stonehenge astronomical calendar. He charted 165 positions of stones and holes at Stonehenge and fed the data into a computer that could line up these positions with points and events in the bowl of the sky. Nothing seemed to line up with stars or planets, but Hawkins found many sightings that lined up with sun and moon positions at different times of the year. Different stones and doorways of trilithons lined up perfectly with equinoxes for both the sun and moon throughout the year. Hawkins also said that by moving counting stones around the circle of the 56 Aubrey Holes the priests could predict lunar eclipses. In 1966 Hawkins stated, "I think I have demonstrated beyond reasonable doubt that the monument was deliberately, accurately, and skillfully oriented to the sun and the moon."[48]

Many respected Stonehenge experts vigorously disagreed and continue to disagree today. They point out that coincidence could explain the Stonehenge alignments, since a sight line toward the sky is bound to hit something. Also, they find errors in Hawkins's reconstruction of the fallen and missing parts of the monument. Stover said of Hawkins's theory, "The whole idea is manifestly absurd."[49] Atkinson derisively deemed Hawkins's theory "Moonshine."[50] Nevertheless, other archaeoastronomers continue to argue for Stonehenge as a celestial observatory. Some use different alignments, and others assign different meanings

> ## " QUOTE "
>
> "My working hypothesis has gradually developed over the past two years: If I can see any alignment, general relationship or use for the various parts of Stonehenge then these facts were also known to the builders."
>
> —Scientist Gerald Hawkins.

to the stones and holes. In 1982 M.W. Postins, for example, argued that the 5 trilithons represented the 5 planets that can be seen with the unaided human eye. Fred Hoyle, an astronomer in England, said that the real observatory was Stonehenge I. The Aubrey Holes predicted lunar eclipses with great accuracy, while the standing stones were perhaps of more religious meaning.

John North, a modern archaeoastronomer, is certain that Stonehenge was a lunar observatory and says that errors in other archaeoastronomers' theories are due to the fact that they were observing alignments from the wrong place. He says people should observe the lunar eclipses from outside the monument, looking in. Even if Stonehenge was not an observatory, most experts do agree that there are solar alignments at Stonehenge that could have had religious significance.

It Was a City or Hospital

Stover, however, believes that Stonehenge was part of a city and was the election court for kings. Perhaps the king's power and authority were increased by the religious aspects of Stonehenge. Perhaps great celebratory banquets were held when the king was crowned there. Maybe the burials around Stonehenge are of kings, princes, and honored warriors. The trilithons, according to Stover, are monuments to dead and living honored nobles.

In 2006 archeologist Timothy Darvill proposed a different interpretation of Stonehenge. He suggested that it was a healing place where sick and injured people went to be cured by the magic stones. Darvill points out that many of the graves around Stonehenge held people with illnesses or injuries. Also, many of them were not from the area of the Salisbury Plain. Scientists have studied the teeth of these skeletons and discovered that some came from Wales or Ireland. One skeleton, known as the Amesbury Archer, came from Switzerland. Why would people travel to Stonehenge from so far away and be buried there? Darvill says people made pilgrimages to Stonehenge as ill people do today to Lourdes to pray to be healed.

The true purpose of Stonehenge probably will always remain a mystery. Most experts suggest multiple purposes and feel sure that at least one of them was religion. Ignorance of the intent of the Stonehenge people, however, has not stopped generations of people from using Stonehenge in their own way.

CHAPTER 6

Stonehenge's Destiny

Archeological digs in and around Stonehenge usually yield more than Neolithic/Bronze Age artifacts. Before the diggers get to that ancient depth, they unearth all sorts of proof of the generations of people who visited Stonehenge before them. When Hawley dug under the Slaughter Stone in 1919, one of his first finds was a bottle of port wine. It had been buried in 1801 by an earlier digger, William Cunnington, as a gift for future archeologists to discover. (Unfortunately for Hawley, the cork in the bottle had rotted away, and so the wine was no longer any good.)

Centuries of Visitor Evidence

Cunnington was neither the first nor the last to leave something behind at Stonehenge. Stonehenge seems to have drawn the living to its environment ever since its builders abandoned it, and the monument is littered with signs of previous visits. Pieces of pottery from the Iron Age (500 to 0 B.C.) have been dug up at Stonehenge. In 1901 archeologist William Gowland conducted a dig at Stonehenge. In the first layers of soil, reports Chippindale, he found "abundant stone chips and flint fragments, clay-pipe stems, pieces of broken crockery, bottles and glass, together with pins, buttons, and other rubbish of obviously recent date."[51] He also found 10 coins from the Roman era and a penny from the time of George III. Chippindale says the finds are proof of hundreds of years of sightseeing and other visits.

Hawley also found Roman pottery chips during his 1919 dig. He dug up British coins from the Elizabethan era and even a cartridge case from World War I. Some experts believe the oldest trash from the Roman occupation and Iron Age indicates that the monument was used as a religious site by later people. They suggest that local chiefs could have used Stonehenge for their own celebrations. But most scientists say that Stonehenge was left alone by later generations except for curious tourists and passersby. Even the Romans seemed unwilling to disturb it or use it for their own purposes.

A Perfect Living Space

In the eighteenth century Stonehenge became a refuge for a different sort of visitor. English blackbirds, called daws, took to nesting in the nooks and crannies of the megaliths. In 1768 historian Gilbert White wrote in a letter to a friend, "These birds deposit their nests in the interstices between the upright and the impost stones of that amazing work of antiquity: which circumstance alone speaks the prodigious height of the upright stones, that they should be tall enough to secure those nests from the annoyance of shepherd-boys, who are always idling around that place."[52]

"Yeah, Yeah, Yeah"

In their 1965 movie *Help!* the Beatles are seen performing with Stonehenge behind them. Stonehenge has been a part of the music culture for decades. Also in the 1960s Richie Havens named an album *Stonehenge*. In 1975 the heavy metal band Spinal Tap recorded a song called "Stonehenge" that described the monument as a magic place where banshees and demons live. Black Sabbath used a mock Stonehenge set onstage. Ayreon's song "And the Druids Turned to Stone" in the 2000 album *Universal Migrator Part I: The Dream Sequencer,* is a fantasy about druids changed to stone and magically becoming Stonehenge.

Other animals have used Stonehenge as a haven. In 2004 badgers began digging homes in the burial mounds around Stonehenge. They destroyed archeological artifacts and disturbed ancient bones. Distressed, some British suggested killing the badgers before they destroyed more of the ancient site, but badgers are protected by law in Britain. The government resorted to moving some of the badgers to new areas and excluding others with a wire fence through which the badgers cannot dig. So far this approach has stopped some of the badgers, but it has not prevented all of them from claiming Stonehenge for themselves.

Excursions Among the Ruins

People have claimed the right to Stonehenge, too, and sometimes done even more damage to the monument than animals ever could. In the 19th century Stonehenge became the fashionable place for Victorian excursions and picnics. Stonehenge was still privately owned then, but "guardians" were appointed in an effort to protect Stonehenge from being loved to destruction. The guardians were to enforce the following rules:

> To see no damage is done to the stones and the grass. To ascertain the names and addresses of any persons so doing and not to allow visitors to picnic inside the stones, nor light fires inside the ditch. Visitors are requested not to put marks or names on the stones. No picketing or feeding of horses allowed between the stones and the ditch. Visitors not to leave rubbish.[33]

The rules were definitely needed but not very successful. People visited Stonehenge in groups traveling in omnibuses and wagonettes. They scribbled their names on the stones, and children used the fallen ones as sliding boards. Young men showed off their strength and daring by climbing to the tops of the megaliths. Broken bottles, chicken bones, and old newspapers were dropped everywhere. Rats and mice moved in and lived on the litter left by human visitors. One year a man carefully carved

Did You Know?

In the nineteenth century Stonehenge became the fashionable place for Victorian excursions and picnics.

"Bridger 1866" into a sarsen stone. Tourists brought hammers with them so as to chip off a piece of rock as a souvenir of the day. Enterprising locals often carried pieces of stones in their pockets to sell to the tourists, but many broke off pieces for themselves "so as to be sure they were genuine."[54]

The gentry of the period objected to all the mess, but they did not leave Stonehenge alone either. By train or private carriage, they arrived at Stonehenge for parties. Queen Victoria's son Leopold brought friends to Stonehenge for a picnic and had his picture taken lolling beside the meal under the megaliths. Stonehenge was the fashionable place to go. Prime Minister William Gladstone visited and later described Stonehenge as "a noble and awful relic, telling much and telling that it conceals more."[55]

Art Claims Stonehenge

Stonehenge was a place for rowdy partying for some, especially at the summer solstice, but it was a place of awe and reverence for many. It seemed full of mystery, meaning, and romance. In 1891 Thomas Hardy used Stonehenge in his novel *Tess of the D'Urbervilles.* As Tess flees from justice after murdering her lover, she seeks refuge at Stonehenge and is arrested there. Other Victorian novelists made Stonehenge the setting for tragic deaths or God's retribution for sins and immorality. One Stonehenge poem, written by Thomas Stokes Salmon begins:

> "Wrap't in the veil of time's unbroken gloom
> Obscure as death, and silent as the tomb
> Where cold oblivion holds her dusky reign
> Frowns the dark pile on Sarum's lonely plain."[56]

Stonehenge was a dark and eerie place of mystery for many

Some people connect Stonehenge with UFOs and alien visitations. Some even suggest that Stonehenge and Britain's other stone circles are all part of a vast network that includes ancient monuments and structures throughout the world.

in these romantic times. Yet everyone felt they had a right to be there, and the awe did not prevent the ongoing destruction.

Fights for the Rights to Stonehenge

During the twentieth century the visits continued. The destruction slowed as Stonehenge was taken over by the government for preservation, but it did not stop. Britain's National Trust tried to control the ways people used Stonehenge. The trust built parking lots and public restrooms and added a fence around the monument itself to keep visitors at a distance. The New Age druids, however, were not the only people to claim the right to use Stonehenge as they wished. During the 1960s war protesters used the monument as the perfect venue to advance their own agendas. They sprayed graffiti slogans on the monument such as "Ban the Bomb." In 1969, when the druids held their solstice ceremonies at Stonehenge, hippies, political anarchists, and other free spirits crashed through the fence and overwhelmed the rituals. The midsummer gatherings grew out of control, despite the best efforts of the British police. Finally, in the early 1980s Britain banned Stonehenge festivals altogether and allowed no access to the monument. The government was determined to preserve Stonehenge as a national treasure. The decision provoked outrage among solstice celebrants and festival goers. They believed that Stonehenge belonged to them.

In 1985 Stonehenge was the scene of a terrible clash between New Agers and the police that came to be known as "The Battle of the Bean Field." In the summer of that year about 600 people got together in a caravan of some 140 vehicles to try to get into, or at least close to, Stonehenge. They wanted to have their festival. Most of them were free spirits and hippies who lived in the vans and buses they drove. Whole families rode in the caravan toward Stonehenge. The police were expecting them and had set up an exclusion zone in a 4-mile perimeter (6.4km) around Stonehenge. The caravan was stopped by police about 7 miles (11km) from Stonehenge. No one is really sure about what happened next. Police moved in and smashed windows and arrested the drivers.

Other caravan members tried to escape by driving into a nearby field. They stayed there for about eight hours, negotiating with police but refusing to leave the area.

Violence erupted. Police deny it, but witnesses say the police became brutal. They attacked and destroyed vehicles; they chased the terrified caravan members on foot into a nearby bean field and beat and arrested them. A journalist named Nick Davies observed the horrible scene. Later he reported, "They [the riot police] were like flies around rotten meat, and there was no question of trying to make a lawful arrest. They crawled all over, truncheons flailing, hitting anybody they could reach. It was extremely violent and very sickening."[57] Other witnesses reported that the police threw things at the travelers, set their vehicles on fire, and clubbed people even though they were holding babies in their arms. Several people were injured and 537 were arrested.

Eventually, all the arrested people were released uncharged, but Britain was horrified by the incident and determined to prevent a recurrence. In 1998 the government began allowing New Age pagans and druids limited access to Stonehenge at certain times of the year. By 2000 Stonehenge was opened to the public for celebrations of the solstices and equinoxes. The gatherings are heavily monitored by police, but they are calm and unobtrusive. Most of the New Agers try to help maintain order. They encourage each other to respect the site and never to climb on the stones. Touching the megaliths and a "stoney hug"[58] are okay.

Stonehenge for Aliens

For druids and hippies, Stonehenge is a place of peace and love now, but other people see it as mystic and eerie. Some of these people connect Stonehenge with UFOs and alien visitations. A few of them claim to have seen UFOs over Stonehenge themselves. One of the strangest stories about Stonehenge took place in 1957. It was retold in 1999 on a Russian UFO Web site this way:

> In August 1957, a war game was held between the London garrison and the Royal Guards from Liverpool [at Stonehenge]. According to the battle's conditions, the defending side (the London garrison) was equipped with five Centurion tanks. The tanks performed a defensive role: they maneuvered and fired at the center of the area. When the tanks were getting ready for the combat mission, the crew of one of the tanks reported that they saw a large, silver, cigar-shaped object; they reported that the tank was ready to open fire. After the report, no more information could be obtained about the tank, and none of its traces could be found. The tank simply disappeared.[59]

One man, Arthur Shuttlewood, reported another UFO sighting at Stonehenge in 1968. He said the ship disappeared into the monument and then became "a ring of fire that evidently shot from the stones themselves, whereupon the UFO fled upwards from our curious approach."[60] UFOs were reported over Stonehenge again in 1977. This time they were glowing lights that hovered and zigzagged around the megaliths before they disappeared.

Intergalactic Claims

People who believe that Earth has been visited by aliens sometimes argue that aliens built Stonehenge. They suggest that Stonehenge and Britain's other stone circles are all part of a vast network that includes ancient monuments and structures throughout the world. These relics all look as if they were planned to be seen from the sky. Author John Cowie says,

> They may have been points in an elaborate intergalactic compass, sextant or star map. They could have been used as links in an interstellar communications network. They may have been constructed to help the Alien Visitor fix its position in relation to the other planets in the galaxy or its own planet so that it would be able to chart a route when it wanted to leave Earth.[61]

Cowie supposes that the "Alien Visitor" organized the primitive tribes around Stonehenge to build the monument. He also thinks it is possible that the aliens were able to levitate the stones, as Merlin did in the old tale, to bring them to the Salisbury Plain.

Many groups of people believe that Cowie is right about an alien link to Stonehenge. Others believe that Stonehenge has strange magnetic powers of healing, as the ancients believed so long ago. All of these people treasure Stonehenge as their link to ancient peoples and experiences in humanity's past. Stonehenge is seen as a mystical place by thousands of people today.

Modern Tourism

Of course, most people think of Stonehenge as an ancient wonder of construction to be visited and admired. All the wonderment put

Stonehenge's fate at risk in the past, but today the British government as well as private preservation groups work to ensure that the site remains protected. Concerned citizens groups also fight to return Stonehenge and its environment to a more natural state.

Modern Stonehenge is a World Heritage site managed by the British government's English Heritage Commission. Britain's National Trust now owns thousands of acres around Stonehenge and controls any development in the area. Stonehenge itself is protected by fences, and visitors must pay a fee to tour the area and see the monument. However, much of the site is already crisscrossed by roads and highways. Farmers have plowed up many acres around Stonehenge and planted crops. In 1999 English Heritage, with the help of private foundations such as Save Stonehenge, published "The Stonehenge Master Plan." It recommended building a tunnel as access to the Stonehenge site and closing the roadways and restoring the land to a natural condition. It also proposed buying up farmers' land and holding it in trust as part of the Stonehenge World Heritage site. It suggested that people should be encouraged to tour all the areas around Stonehenge, but by walking or on bicycles. Some private groups proposed a train to Stonehenge so as to do away with cars and parking lots altogether. Others suggested moving parking lots well away from Stonehenge and busing people to the actual site. None of these ideas has been easy to implement. Some are fought over bitterly by different interested groups.

A New Plan—a New Controversy

By 2007 Save Stonehenge was outraged and upset by the government's implementation of the plan. It does include a tunnel passing the Stonehenge site. The tunnel would be 1.3 miles (2km) long. But 6 miles (9.7km) of a new four-lane highway would bisect the rest of the World Heritage site. Earth would be bulldozed and artifacts destroyed, says the Save Stonehenge Web site. It complains, "Stonehenge is threatened by [this] massive and highly destructive road-building scheme."[62] Some British lawmakers agree that the plan is a poor one, and many are distressed that no decisions have been implemented to improve Stonehenge, even though it has been 10 years since the Master Plan was presented. Finances and differing opinions both interfere with government plans to save Stonehenge sites for future generations.

While groups such as Save Stonehenge protest current plans, the government and the National Trust believe the plan will accomplish much to protect and preserve Stonehenge while still being financially feasible. The name of the Master Plan has been changed to the Stonehenge Project. The Stonehenge Project's Web site says, "The Stonehenge Project is designed to improve the setting and interpretation of Stonehenge. It will remove the sights and sounds of the roads and traffic from the area near the Stones, recreate chalk downland from arable farmland and transform the visitor experience with better access to the landscape and a new world class visitor centre."[63] Most people are pleased by the idea of relocating farmers and creating a visitor center, but the new proposed highway to replace existing roads is very controversial.

Stonehenge for the Ages

On one thing, however, almost everyone agrees: Stonehenge is the rightful heritage of all the world's people and must always be protected. Every year more than 800,000 people experience the wonder of visiting Stonehenge. It is an international treasure, beloved today and destined to inspire and astonish millions of future visitors with its mysterious power.

NOTES

Introduction: Silent Stones

1. Bernard Cornwell, "Bernard Cornwell on *Stonehenge*," HarperCollins: Author Interview. www.harpercollins.com.
2. Quoted in Cornwell, "Bernard Cornwell on *Stonehenge*."

Chapter 1: Mysterious Stonehenge

3. Quoted in "Stonehenge: A Megalithic Mystery," New-age. www.new-age.co.uk.
4. Quoted in "Stonehenge: A Megalithic Mystery."
5. Quoted in Gerald S. Hawkins, *Stonehenge Decoded*. New York: Barnes and Noble, 1993, p. 4.
6. Quoted in Hawkins, *Stonehenge Decoded*, p. 4.
7. Quoted in Christopher Chippindale, *Stonehenge Complete*. Ithaca, NY: Cornell University Press, 1983, p. 48.
8. Quoted in Hawkins, *Stonehenge Decoded*, p. 12.
9. Quoted in Hawkins, *Stonehenge Decoded*, p. 24.
10. Quoted in Hawkins, *Stonehenge Decoded*, p. 24.
11. Quoted in Hawkins, *Stonehenge Decoded*, p. 25.

Chapter 2: The People of Stonehenge

12. Rodney Castleden, *The Stonehenge People*. New York: Routledge, 1993, p. 260.
13. Castleden, *The Stonehenge People*, p. 199.
14. Chippindale, *Stonehenge Complete*, p. 267.
15. Colin Burgess, *The Age of Stonehenge*. Edison, NJ: Castle, 2003, p. 333.
16. Quoted in Leon Stover, *Stonehenge City*. Jefferson, NC: McFarland, 2003, p. 36.
17. Hawkins, *Stonehenge Decoded*, p. 71.

Chapter 3: A Culture of Circles and Rings

18. Quoted in Chippindale, *Stonehenge Complete*, p. 188.
19. Quoted in Helen Thomas, "Seeking the Secrets of Stonehenge," September 1, 2006. www.thisiswiltshire.co.uk.
20. Quoted in Thomas, "Seeking the Secrets of Stonehenge."
21. Quoted in Morien Institute, "The Wooden Pre-Megalithic Structure Discovered at Stanton Drew." www.morien-institute.org.
22. Hawkins, *Stonehenge Decoded*, p. 84.
23. Castleden, *The Stonehenge People*, p. 236.
24. Stover, *Stonehenge City*, pp. 59–60.
25. Castleden, *The Stonehenge People*, p. 185.
26. Terence Meaden, *Stonehenge: The Secret of the Solstice*. London: Souvenir, 1997, p. 19.
27. Meaden, *Stonehenge*, p. 86.

Chapter 4: Celts and Stonehenge

28. David Loxley, "Ancient Order of Druids," *Festival Eye Magazine*, 1988. www.phreak.co.uk.
29. Quoted in Hawkins, *Stonehenge Decoded*, pp. 14–15.
30. Quoted in Hawkins, *Stonehenge Decoded*, pp. 19–20.
31. Quoted in Matthew Schneider, "'Wrung by Sweet Enforcement': Druid Stones and the Problem of Sacrifice in British Romanticism." *Anthropoetics*, vol. 2, no. 2, January 1997. www.anthropoetics.ucla.edu.
32. Quoted in Norton Online Archive, "The Romantic Period: 1785–1830," chap. 6. www2.wwnorton.com.
33. Quoted in Icons: A Portrait of England, "Jerusa-

lem." www.icons.org.uk.

34. Quoted in Isaac Bonwits, "The Story of Druidism: History, Legend, and Lore," United Ancient Order of Druids. www.neopagan.net.

35. Philip Carr-Gomm, *Druid Mysteries*, Order of Bards, Ovates, and Druids." www.druidry.org.

36. Carr-Gomm, *Druid Mysteries*.

37. Stover, *Stonehenge City*, p. 11.

38. Stover, *Stonehenge City*, p. 19.

39. Carr-Gomm, *Druid Mysteries*.

40. Hawkins, *Stonehenge Decoded*, p. 18.

Chapter 5: Exploring the "Why" of Stonehenge

41. Castleden, *The Stonehenge People*, p. 151.

42. Meaden, *Stonehenge: The Secret of the Solstice*, p. 13.

43. Hawkins, *Stonehenge Decoded*, p. 55.

44. Meaden, *Stonehenge: The Secret of the Solstice*, p. 95.

45. Meaden, *Stonehenge: The Secret of the Solstice*, p. 112.

46. Hawkins, *Stonehenge Decoded*, pp. 146–47.

47. Stover, *Stonehenge City*, p. 28.

48. Quoted in Paul Aron, *Unsolved Mysteries of History*. New York: Barnes and Noble, 2003, p. 15.

Chapter 6: Stonehenge's Destiny

49. Chippindale, *Stonehenge Complete*, pp. 167–68.

50. "Letter XXI, To Thomas Pennant Esquire, Nov. 28, 1768," in Gilbert White, *The Natural History of Selbourne*, section 4. Seattle: World Wide School, May 1999. www.worldwideschool.org.

51. Quoted in Chippindale, *Stonehenge Complete*, p. 159.

52. Quoted in Chippindale, *Stonehenge Complete*, pp. 159–60.

53. Quoted in Chippindale, *Stonehenge Complete*, p. 152.

54. Quoted in Chippindale, *Stonehenge Complete*, p. 150.

55. Quoted in Tony Thompson, "Twenty Years After, Mystery Still Clouds Battle of the Beanfield," *Observer* (London), June 12, 2005. http://observer.guardian.co.uk.

56. New-Age, "Stonehenge Summer and Winter Solstice Pictures." www.new-age.co.uk.

57. Stig Agermose, "Stonehenge a Magnet for UFOs?" Pravda.RU, Virtually Strange.net. www.virtuallystrange.net.

58. Quoted in Chippindale, *Stonehenge Complete*, p. 245.

59. John Cowie, "Crop Circles: The Live Link to Our Extraterrestrial Ancestors?" 2002. www.sayer.abel.co.uk.

60. Save Stonehenge! "World Heritage Site Threatened by Roadbuilding Scheme!" July 5, 2007. www.savestonehenge.org.uk.

61. Stonehenge Project, "Welcome to the Stonehenge Project." www.thestonehengeproject.org.

Books

DK Publishing, *Early Humans*. New York: Dorling Kindersley, 2005.

William W. Lace, *Stonehenge*. San Diego, CA: Lucent, 2003.

Caroline Malone and Nancy Stone Bernard, *Digging for the Past: Stonehenge*. New York: Oxford University Press, 2002.

Tom McGowan, *Giant Stones and Earth Mounds*. Brookfield, CT: Millbrook, 2000.

Michael Woods and Mary B. Woods, *Ancient Computing: From Counting to Calendars*. Minneapolis: Runestone, 2000.

Web Sites

Archaeoastronomy.com (www.archaeoastronomy.com). Earth's clock, the solstices and equinoxes, and how archaeoastronomy helps scientists understand ancient knowledge.

Mysterious Britain (www.mysteriousbritain.co.uk). The myths, legends, and mysteries of Britain's many weird, paranormal places.

New-Age.co.uk (www.new-age.co.uk). Photos and descriptions of New Age festivals at Stonehenge and other sacred sites in Britain.

Stonehenge.co.uk (www.stonehenge.co.uk). A guide to everything Stonehenge, including visits.

Stonehenge Riverside Project (www.shef.ac.uk/archaeology/research/stonehenge). Every university involved in the project has its own Web site. This one from the University of Sheffield provides the latest information about the newest digs and includes links to other news.

ĬNDEX

About the Author

Toney Allman holds degrees from Ohio State University and the University of Hawaii. She currently lives in rural Virginia, right beside a bean field. She enjoys gardening and walking, as well as learning about the world and writing nonfiction books for students.